THE STORY OF THE
NOOSPHERE

THE STORY OF THE

NOOSPHERE

Brian Thomas Swimme

&

Monica DeRaspe-Bolles

Illustrations by Sebastian Swimme

ORBIS BOOKS

Maryknoll, New York 10545

Founded in 1970, Orbis Books endeavors to publish works that enlighten the mind, nourish the spirit, and challenge the conscience. The publishing arm of the Maryknoll Fathers and Brothers, Orbis seeks to explore the global dimensions of the Christian faith and mission, to invite dialogue with diverse cultures and religious traditions, and to serve the cause of reconciliation and peace. The books published reflect the views of their authors and do not represent the official position of the Maryknoll Society. To learn more about Maryknoll and Orbis Books, please visit our website at www.orbisbooks.com

Manufactured in the United States of America

Library of Congress Cataloging-in-Publication Data

Names: Swimme, Brian, author. | DeRaspe-Bolles, Monica, author. | Swimme,
   Sebastian, illustrator.
Title: The story of the noosphere / Brian Thomas Swimme and
   Monica DeRaspe-Bolles ; illustrations by Sebastian Swimme.
Description: Maryknoll, NY : Orbis Books, [2024] | Includes
   bibliographical references. | Summary: "The story of cosmic
   evolution through the lens of Teilhard de Chardin's philosophy of
   evolution"— Provided by publisher.
Identifiers: LCCN 2024013735 (print) | LCCN 2024013736
   (ebook) | ISBN 9781626985940 (hardcover) |
   ISBN 9798888660508 (epub)
Subjects: LCSH: Evolution—Religious aspects—Catholic Church.
   | Human evolution—Religious aspects—Catholic Church. |
   Cosmology. | Teilhard de Chardin, Pierre.
Classification: LCC BX1795.E85 S95 2024 (print) |
   LCC BX1795.E85 (ebook) | DDC 231.7/652—dc23/
   eng/20240528
LC record available at https://lccn.loc.gov/2024013735
LC ebook record available at https://lccn.loc.gov/2024013736

Dedicated to

Professor Francis Cousens,

our teacher and friend

CONTENTS

CLASSICAL

MODERN

ACKNOWLEDGMENTS

The Story of the Noosphere is a project of Human Energy (humanenergy.io), a public benefit nonprofit organization that focuses on scientific and interdisciplinary research on the future of human collective consciousness, steered by a team of scientists, scholars, and philosophers representing international universities and organizations at the forefront of research. Human Energy positions its work in the lineage of thought inaugurated by the French Jesuit scientist Pierre Teilhard de Chardin. One hundred years ago, Teilhard began publishing his radical and disruptive yet vital and creative scientific theory of evolution. Though science largely ignored his work, discoveries since the mid-twentieth century have bolstered Teilhard's vision and pushed the criticisms of his detractors aside. A key scientist in this profound reversal is the Belgian physical chemist Ilya Prigogine, with his extensive investigations into the time-developmental nature of the universe. To our knowledge, Human Energy is the first organization formed for the sole purpose of researching and disseminating the scientific theory of the noosphere. Our book and YouTube video series of the same name form the heart of Human Energy's effort to disseminate this profound new vision of a time-developing universe.

We are grateful to Ben Kacyra, who, over a long life, has kept alive his passion to deepen the scientific study of Teilhard's theory of the noosphere and to bring Teilhard's vision of humanity's unity to a larger audience. From the beginning, Ben collaborated to develop the overall form and focus of our work and conceived the crucial idea that our narrative be structured using the eight aspects of the noosphere. We are grateful he entrusted the writing to us, confident that our work would advance Human Energy's mission to bring a renewed sense of meaning and purpose to our increasingly interconnected society.

In the writing of this book and the video scripts, Monica DeRaspe-Bolles and Brian Thomas Swimme have benefited from the research of Human Energy scientists and scholars, including Terrence Deacon, Department of Anthropology at the University of California at Berkeley; Sheila Hassell Hughes, Dean of Liberal

Studies at St. Mary's College of California; Wolfgang Leidhold, professor of political philosophy at the University of Cologne; Francis Heylighen, director of the transdisciplinary Center Leo Apostel at the Free University of Brussels; Parham Pourdavood, data scientist and neuroscience researcher; Shima Beigi, resilience scientist and founder of Mindfulness Engineering; Clément Vidal, researcher for the Global Brain Institute at the Free University of Brussels; David Sloan Wilson, a biologist at Binghamton University; and Marta Lenartowicz, interdisciplinary researcher and educator at the Free University of Brussels.

As our book was informed in part by our video series that preceded it, we take this opportunity to thank its production team: executive producers Ben and Barbara Kacyra, producer and director Devin O'Dea, editor Abe Costanza, sound engineer Matthew Harting, associate producer Jason Jakaitis, and cinematographers Luke Walker and Kisa Knight.

We are immensely grateful for our conversations over time about Teilhard and the noosphere. Our interlocutors include Ashton Arnoldy, Theo Badashi, Bruce Bochte, David J. Bolles, Jeff Booth, Josefina Burgos, Paul Caringella, Carolyn Cooke, Francis Cousens, Bruce Damer, Ilia Delio, Robert Del Tredici, John DeRaspe, Christoph Ferstad, Abre Fournier, Matthew Fox, Linda Gibler, John Grim, John Haught, Louis Herman, Alan Honick, Shelli Joye, Ayeh Kashani, Sean Kelly, Joseph Lamb, Laura Lee, Ari Makridakis, Robert McDermott, Guy Reid, Paul Robear, Matthew Segall, Hiroko Shiota, Boris Shoshitaishvili, Matthew Switzer, Richard Tarnas, Mary Evelyn Tucker, Brian Wheeler, Jason Wirth, and Richard Wormstall.

And finally, it is our joy to thank our highly professional team at Orbis Books, the publisher of several Teilhardian works before ours. Orbis Books shares our hope that Teilhard's vision of the noosphere will enter ever more deeply into humanity throughout the twenty-first century.

INVITATION

To understand what it means to be human, we need to think in terms of the whole journey of our universe and Earth. Considered from the point of view of the dynamics of Earth's evolution, humanity is a singular species. For instance, of the estimated 66,800 vertebrate species alive today, 66,799 have evolved in the same way: distant ancestors spread out and diversified into new species. A thoroughly researched example is that of the mammals. Millions of years ago, some tree shrews fanned out and began the long process of evolution into horses, rhinoceroses, monkeys, bats, and whales. Humanity is the one exception to this dynamic of organic evolution. As humans spread over the surface of Earth, instead of diversifying into new species, they invented tools and amassed a shared cultural heredity that enabled them to maintain the same anatomy and physiology for three hundred thousand years. Instead of speciating, humans folded back on themselves and complexified into villages, cities, and civilizations.

Our book explores the complexity created by human thought and activity. Pierre Teilhard de Chardin named this complex collective the "noosphere" and described it as the "thinking sphere" of Earth. He speculated that the noosphere was a living entity, one best understood as a superorganism. Just as an animal's mind is evoked by the synergy of the various cells of its body, so too the noosphere—with its planetary mind and planetary nervous system—is evoked by the synergistic relationships of thinking humans throughout the planet.

Evolutionary Time

To assert that a new living, planetary entity is emerging out of humanity's actions is radical for modern minds. We are not practiced at thinking in terms of evolutionary time. Our cultural habit is to dwell in the temporal framework of our nation or our religion, but more is needed to take in the full creativity of evolutionary time. From the perspective of our time-developmental universe, our moment is the third of three major transformations that have taken place over the last fourteen billion years.

In the first transformation, primordial plasma, composed of elementary particles, transformed into stars, galaxies, and planets. The elementary particles did not change. They did nothing more than enter into new relationships with each other. That alone empowered them to construct two trillion galaxies. A similar action took place when molten rock transformed into living organisms. As before, the elements which brought this about—oxygen, carbon, phosphorus, and so on—did not change. The chemical elements entered into new relationships, giving birth to the first living cells. Now, in our moment, the third metamorphosis is taking place. Right before our eyes, a living Earth is transforming into a thinking Earth. This is Teilhard's great insight: The noosphere is arising through the deepening relationships of humans all around the planet. Humanity is now awakening to its cosmological task of bringing the noosphere to full consciousness.

Imagination

The challenge of our time is to develop an imagination that can see beyond the chaos to the creative processes at play in our world. A different form of humanity is coming forth, one that seeks to live in harmony with the entire Earth community by aligning itself with the fundamental principles of Earth and the universe. To assist in awakening our imaginations, we ground our thinking in contemporary science and express the noospheric vision using poetic stanzas enlivened by visual art. There is no infallible program for marching into the future. We will find our creative pathways by opening our minds, deepening our imaginations, and embracing evolution's trial-and-error process.

The Eight Aspects of the Noosphere

To narrate the story of the noosphere's emergence, we consider four eras of humanity's evolution: the Paleolithic, Neolithic, Classical, and Modern. In each of these eras, we examine humanity's development in terms of eight interrelated aspects: heredity, tools, reflective consciousness, communication, population, trade, cerebralization, and convergence. The four eras form the sections of the book, and chapters 1–8 of each section correspond to the aspects. We finish our invitation with a brief sketch of the aspects.

1. Heredity

The universe remembers its creative achievements and passes them down, generation to generation. Cultural heredity is the way humanity develops through time. We are born into already existing structures bequeathed to us by our ancestors.

2. Tools

Tools are the stone, wood, metallic, or electronic devices invented by humans for entering new relationships within the Earth community. The tools of the noosphere are evolving extensions of human sensation and human will.

3. Reflective Consciousness

Consciousness is the deepening awareness of our participation in cosmic evolution. Human consciousness deepened with the awareness of being a self. In contemporary societies, a great leap is taking place. Human consciousness is awakening to its participation in a collective, planetary mind.

4. Communication

Communication is the process whereby the parts of the whole establish relationships and enable the whole to complexify. Yes, we are in communication within the human realm, but we are also in communication with every level, from atoms to life to the expanding galaxies. Humanity is the space where the universe deepens its relationships in conscious self-awareness.

5. Population

The complexity of a human population determines the possibilities for human life. Number is critical. When groups of humans gather around a single idea, they amplify potencies that were not available previously, thereby deepening society's complexity.

6. Trade

Trade is the exchange of goods and the deepening of mutuality. Recognizing and satisfying the desires of our trading partners is the pathway into the future. Interconnectivity established by trade has led to a spectacular rise in the quality of human life.

7. Cerebralization

Whereas tools are the bodylike aspect of the noosphere, cerebralization is the corresponding mindlike aspect. Human thought is externalized in symbols, law codes, and cultural conventions that endure and evolve through time. Taken together, humanity and its tools form what can be called a "hyperbody," and the process of cerebralization is how the hyperbody survives and thrives as a component of the Earth community.

8. Convergence

When two or more humans—each with their unique inheritance, each with their extensions in the structures of tools and cerebralization—come together through communication and trade and discover a shared understanding and purpose, the result is convergence. Convergence is the noosphere rising.

Our thirty-two chapters tell the story of the noosphere from our four-foot-tall ancestors to the global, collective brain now enveloping the planet. Each short chapter is an invitation to see the noosphere's development through time. Each is whole unto itself. Jump in anywhere and you will feel the sweep of humanity's development into a collective mind. The transformation from a living planet to a thinking Earth will require new conceptions in every field, beginning with a fundamental shift in consciousness. As you read and reflect on the noosphere, you will come to know that we humans are the universe activating a new era of Earth's story.

PALEOLITHIC

1 PALEOLITHIC HEREDITY
The Story and the Campfire

It is astounding to take in humanity's journey,
where we've come from
and where we are.
We began as four-foot-tall apes
feeding on insects and roots,
trembling when the great cats happened by.[1]
And now, after swarming out of Africa,
we find ourselves the dominant species
throughout Earth.[2]

The power that enabled us
to become a new geological force
was symbolic language.
Its creation took place
over a prolonged period,
but considered within the context
of a fourteen-billion-year universe,
the mysterious symbols of language
thundered forth in an instant
and changed Earth forever.

Our ancestors used language to tell stories
during the Paleolithic stage of humanity.

Some anthropologists speculate
our linguistic creativity developed
not only throughout the day's activities,
but also around the campfire
in the dark of night.[3]
In the presence of the flickering flames,
the fire that arose from the wood
ignited another fire
in the human mind.

Imagine a group of our ancestors
after a day spent hunting and foraging.
Their campfire provides warmth and safety.
As they sit sharing food,
the pressures of the day are gone.

A female sits quietly,
her imagination sparked
by the fire's dancing lights.
She remembers a terrifying experience
earlier that day
when she encountered a lion
and called out to her friends.
Out of a desire to connect with her kin,
she mimics the movements of the lion
and makes the same call
she had made earlier
when she was filled with fear.
But this time,
she calls to be bonded
with her community.

The miracle is the moment
her listeners know
they are experiencing the day's events
all over again—
the same terror,
the same relief,
the same thrill.
Telling the story deepens their relations.
The lion is not even there,
but the experience of communion is.
Her story deepens their relations
through its power of making the past present.[4]

When humans found they could express an experience
with sounds coming from their mouths,
they learned to pass knowledge
from one generation to the next.
This capacity was novel in the life world.
Each new generation of lions or antelopes
begins anew with only the skills
their parents had at birth.
But with human language,
knowledge accumulates beyond DNA.
Discoveries made even a hundred generations ago
are layered into the stories
told around a campfire.

Our predators found themselves
confronted by a group mind
far too powerful to compete against.
Our predators became our prey.
For contemporary hunter-gatherers,
such as the Agta in the Philippines,
storytelling is even more valuable than hunting skills.[5]

We have entered a new era of cosmic storytellers.
Humans around the planet
have discovered this new story
of galaxies, stars, black holes,
and deepening cognition.
Though this third story[6]
draws upon vast domains of knowledge
unknown to our ancestors,
the primary purpose remains the same:
the unification of our tribe.

The fire that enabled humans
to encircle Earth
has become a fire in the mind,
the fire of the noosphere.
This new story of the universe
will unite us in the common purpose
of building a planetary human organism,
an envelope of thought
that brings to us
the wisdom of a thousand generations.

2 PALEOLITHIC TOOLS
The Acceleration of Evolution

After 300,000 years of human evolution,
we have become the dominant species
in the Earth community.
How did this happen?
What power enabled us to outcompete
every other species on our planet?
Our understanding of this power
determines our future.

The distinguishing power of the human species
is its ability to accelerate
the processes of evolution.
Tool use in the Paleolithic stage of humanity
initiated the development
of an organized matrix
of human invention outside its body.

Culturally inherited technologies
accelerated human evolution
by a factor of at least one thousand.[7]
If this estimate is accurate,
we can understand how humanity
came to dominate.
No mammal, no fish, no bird
can compete with a species evolving
a thousand times faster than they are.

Fire provides an illustration.
Fire is a power in the universe
that is extremely rare.[8]
There is no fire on the moon.
There is no fire on any other planet
in our solar system.
Earth itself took billions of years
to develop an atmosphere
enabling fire to come forth.
Even with an oxygenated atmosphere,
Earth needed another 360 million years
to evolve a species
that could transform this wild power
into a tool.

Half a million years ago,
humans used fire to harden sticks.
Suddenly, we were capable of hunting
beasts the size of mastodons.
It would have taken a million years
for a primate species to evolve claws
long enough to stalk large animals.
Yet, once the thought
of clawlike weapons
occurred to just one human,
fire-hardened spears were soon a reality
throughout the continents.

With fire as our tool,
we changed the structure of ecosystems.
We set the forest undergrowth on fire
to make it easier for us to hunt.
We burned fields to make them more fertile for our plants.
Primatologists speculate that using fire to cook food
accelerated the expansion of the human brain.[9]
What is beyond dispute
is that cooking with fire
enabled us to feed upon
a diverse set of plants and animals
without having to wait a million years
for our bodies to evolve capacities
for digesting these foods raw.

If you reflect on your actions throughout your day,
you will discover that much of your living
derives from humanity's use of fire.
If we think of fish as a water species,
and birds as the species of the air,
we can begin to see that
humans are a species of fire.

Is there a meaning in the human acceleration of evolution?
Without question.
Fire creates, even as it destroys.
The same fire that enabled humanity
to dominate the other species
launched us into the process
of becoming an enveloping intelligence.

We are coming to understand
that our powerful technologies
are not for domination,
but for building a planetary mind
that will guide the whole Earth community
into a new era of flourishing.

That realization
is the fundamental shift in consciousness
taking place in our time.

PALEOLITHIC REFLECTION
Neotenic Consciousness

⟩ 3

Every culture on Earth
has pondered what it means to be human.
Modern science is no exception.
Science's offering is that
humanity is the unique primate species
that remains childlike throughout its life.

That is the difference that leads to our monumental presence.
We're unique among all primates
because of this childlike nature,
which we name our *neotenic consciousness*.[10]

To understand the origin
of this neotenic consciousness,
we need to think in terms of epigenesis,
the process by which
animals develop from eggs
through phase sequences.

A chimpanzee begins as a fertilized egg,
then transforms into an embryo,
then an infant,
then an adolescent,
and finally an adult.

The big surprise is that
the DNA molecules are the same in each phase.
The DNA of the embryo
is precisely the DNA of the adult.
Genetically identical,
the phases are distinct
because epigenetic pathways
roam about the DNA molecule,
drawing upon one combination of genes
for the embryo,
and a somewhat different combination of genes
for the adult.[11]

Humanity's neotenic consciousness
began six million years ago
when a mutation event
separated humans from chimpanzees.[12]
Those crucial mutations slowed down
the timing of epigenesis,
stretching out the infant and juvenile chimp phases
into the entire life sequence
of the human species.

What was the result of this mutation?
Observe the behavior of any mammalian child,
whether we are speaking of a puppy or a chimp,
and you will note a similar set of traits,
including curiosity, friendliness, and playfulness.[13]
Mammalian children are ready to form relationships
with members of all species.
But as they enter adulthood,
such qualities are typically replaced
by the fixed-action patterns of adulthood
and a more rigid focus on survival.

Humans are different.
All of us have an exceedingly long childhood for learning
and a capacity for play and exploration
that sustains throughout adulthood.[14]
We have the option of maintaining interest
in all animals, not just humans.
Our neotenic consciousness
offers humans the possibility
of caring for every form of life
throughout our lifetimes.

Our childlike core nature,
with its trust, curiosity, and friendliness,
can become the central form
of humanity.
Our neotenic nature
can empower us to become
not only the mind enveloping the planet,
but the heart that embraces the beauty
of all forms of life.

PALEOLITHIC COMMUNICATION
Cosmic Conversations

Recently, a new form of communication
called symbolic communication
has burst forth from Earth's dynamics.
Symbolic communication
is how the universe as a whole
speaks to us.
Understanding the cosmic dimension of language
will activate deep reservoirs of well-being.
Connected to an unwavering source of purpose,
we find the guidance
to navigate our turbulent era.

Symbolic communication is a recent advance
in the universe's development.
In terms of cosmic time,
it is extremely recent.
If we imagine the universe's evolution
as taking place over a single year,
symbolic communication appears
in the last fraction of a second.[15]
Symbolism is so elaborate,
so profound,
it required the whole vast range
of the universe's complexification
to bring it forth.

Cosmogenesis,
the creative advance of the universe,
always involves novel forms of communication.
The construction of galaxies
started with meaningful exchanges
at the quantum level.
Atoms sent out messenger particles,
called gravitons,
that announced to the world,
"I have mass!"[16]
With that quantum proclamation,
the attraction between atoms actuated.
The formation of stars and galaxies was underway.

With life, we find qualitatively new modes of communication.
When a living organism
receives a relevant message,
it changes its form.
Scientists at the University of British Columbia
have discovered that plants
are linked in complex systems
of nurture and support.[17]
When a tree is attacked by insects,
it sends molecular signals
down its roots into fungal networks
that connect to the root systems
of its neighbors.
The messenger molecules say, in effect,
"I am being eaten by caterpillars! Protect yourself!"
In response to the warning,
nearby trees construct and store
toxic chemicals in their leaves.
Caterpillars who ingest the tainted foliage
are immediately repulsed.

Such signaling is widespread in the animal world.
When a chimpanzee spots a predator,
it gives out a particular hoot
to indicate a leopard is nearby.[18]

Humans, too, employ this form of signaling,
but we have learned to do something more.
We began to communicate
about things that are not present.
That is the power of symbolic language.[19]
With symbols,
humans are no longer constrained
to one time and place.
Our ability to escape local time and space
enables us to conceive of larger contexts,
even the universe as a whole.

Consider the radiation of photons
from the cosmic microwave background,
the particles of light
from time's beginning
that shower down on Earth.
These photons showered the first forests.
They showered the dinosaurs.
They showered the chimpanzees.

Then, after billions of years,
along came humans.
Using minds that had been developed
over millennia,
we learned to listen
to the *story* these particles of light
had been telling all along:
the story of how the universe
came forth from a seed,
how the expansion of the universe
led to stars, galaxies, and life.

On the one hand,
these photons are nothing more
than particles of light.
On the other hand,
through human consciousness,
these particles became symbols
that tell the universe's narrative.

This book on the noosphere
is ultimately the universe
speaking to you.
The conditions we present
concerning humanity's development—
our technologies, our trading routes,
our deepening powers to connect—
are facts of human history
that carry immense significance,
symbols that narrate the epic story
of a developing planetary mind,
the noosphere.

Our destinies,
both as individuals and communities,
are woven into
this cosmic conversation.

What could be
more important to know?

PALEOLITHIC POPULATION
The Odyssey of *Homo Erectus*

When members of *Homo erectus*,
the first human species,
emerged in Africa two million years ago,
they found themselves at the start
of a great mission:
to spread out and increase their population
beyond that of any other mammalian group
in all of evolutionary history.[20]

The drive to distribute
over the surface of Earth
was altogether new among primates.
The DNA molecules
of *Homo erectus* and chimpanzees
are 99 percent identical.[21]
Yet, chimps hunkered down
in their African biome
for thirty million years,
while their human cousins
exploded out of Africa
to encircle the globe.

Early humans did not know
why they had to leave Africa.
They would not have been able
to explain what drove them.
Only now can we see
the deeper significance
of their movement
and understand their situation
as homologous to the construction
of a mammalian brain.

In a developing embryo,
fetal cells gather together,
specialize into nerve cells,
and become the mammal's central nervous system.
A similar process took place
with Earth as a whole,
as early humans set out on their odyssey,
encompassed Earth,
and specialized into planetary nerve cells.
Homo erectus left Africa
on a two-million-year journey
to build a brain of brains,
the noosphere.

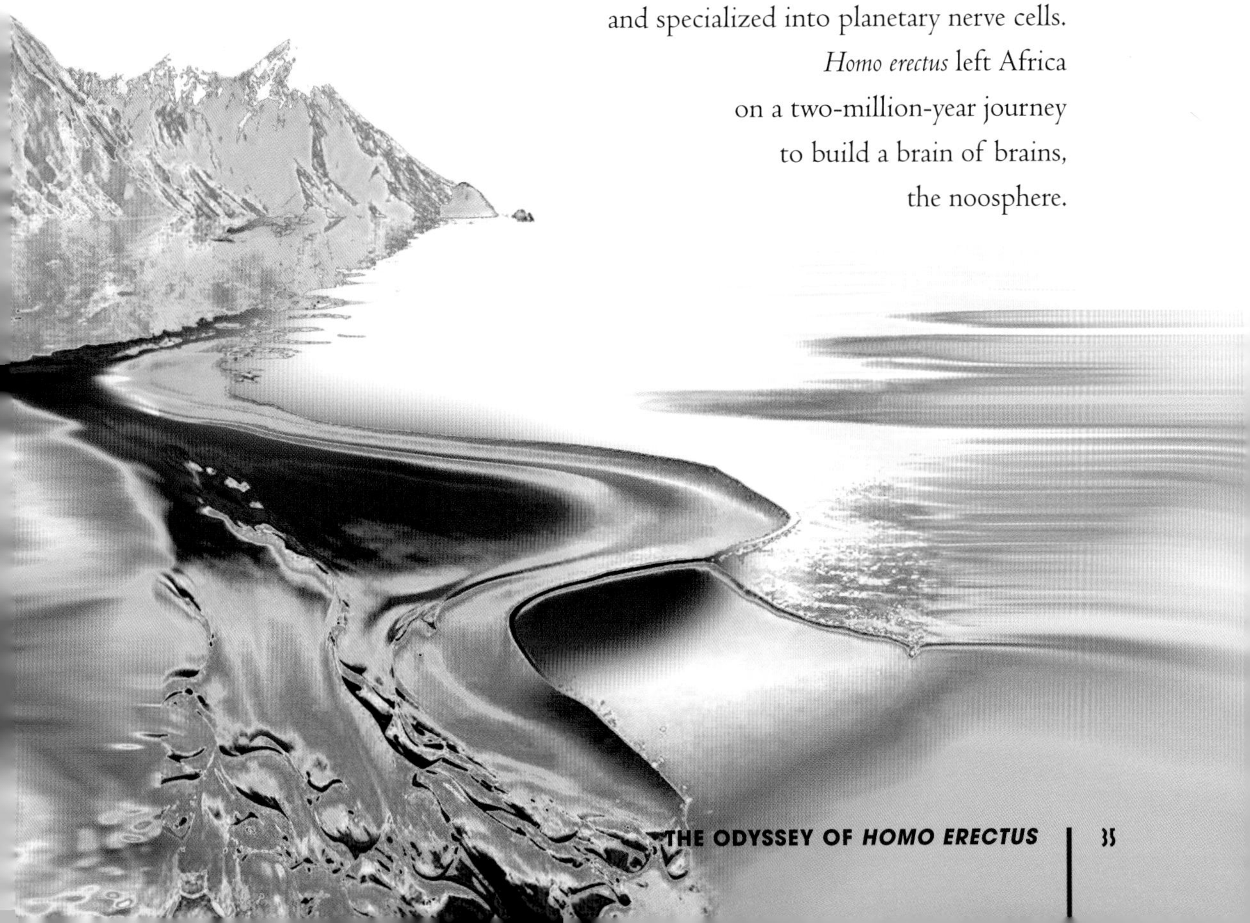

Pause a moment and take in the grandeur of this story.
For two thousand years, Western civilization has celebrated
the heroism of Odysseus
as he made his way about the Mediterranean Sea.
But his heroism pales in comparison
to that of the earliest humans
who left the balmy, African tropics
on a seven-hundred-and-fifty-thousand-year march
to the upper limits of the Asian continent.[22]
When they arrived there,
they found themselves in an ice age
that buried the land in mile-high glaciers.[23]
Even then, they persisted.
Some of their descendants made their way to Australia.
Others hunted the great mastodons at the Arctic Circle,
while others survived
in the snake-infested swamps of North Carolina.

As humans spread over the surface of Earth,
each group burrowed
into the rhythms of its biome.
One group wore the same furs
as the brown bears.
Another group traveled the same routes
as the migrating reindeer.
Still another constructed ritual
wearing the feathers of birds.

In all of this development,
each regional group specialized
as the human form of their biome.
Communication between different human groups
was Earth growing in awareness of its body.

In a developing embryo,
as neurons connect,
there comes a time
when the animal mind awakens.
Earth is in that moment.

Increasingly, we are aware
of the planetary effects of our lives.
With humans densely situated
throughout the planet
and all groups connected
via modern communication systems,
we are beginning to realize we are
the first structures of a planetary brain.

You, by studying the details
of the noosphere's emergence,
become an essential part of the awakening.
The way to proceed is present,
just as it was present in *Homo erectus*.
As we align our ambitions
with the vitality of Earth
and pursue our unique fascinations,
we carry forward the heroic action
of building a planetary mind,
the noosphere.

PALEOLITHIC TRADE
6 Becoming One Another

Though we are similar to other animals
in many ways,
we humans seem to be
the only animal species on Earth
that engages in conscious trade.
This capacity to trade via bartering
has amplified in profound ways
the evolution of humanity
and led to a spectacular rise
in the quality of human life.

Necklaces of perforated seashells
found throughout Africa,
from the Blombos caves in the south,
to the Mediterranean shores in the north,
suggest early humans
were engaged in complex exchange networks
between coastal and inland peoples
as early as seventy to eighty thousand years ago.[24]

Imagine a hypothetical event
in this long-ago time
when two groups of humans
came together to trade.
Travelers from the sea
carry a bundle of shell necklaces.
The hosts who live close to a volcano
possess a great many fire-hardened spears.

The trade occurs
when both sides feel they are getting a good deal.
But what is a good deal?
How many spears are equal to one necklace?

Humans forged agreements
by reflecting on the whole process:
the amount of time it took to make the items,
the difficulty in finding the materials,
the arduous journey required,
and so forth.
Trade is synergistic
in that it brings to each side
what it considered more valuable
than what is exchanged.
The implications for the evolution of humanity
are immense
because trade by bartering
accelerates the development
of both groups.

A fantastic demonstration of this synergy
took place fifty thousand years ago
among Paleolithic humans
who settled throughout the seventeen thousand islands
of the Indonesian seas.

Each island had developed
its own seagoing technology
with unique features of material and technique.
But as trade networks developed throughout Indonesia,
inhabitants of disparate islands
encountered a broader range of inventions
that had surfaced elsewhere.
Naturally enough, the islanders gravitated toward
the most effective techniques and the best materials.

Combining breakthroughs in boat construction
from many separate communities
led to designs capable of long-distance sailing.
Suddenly, they had the capacity
to reach the Australian continent.[25]
No island left to its own ideas
could have matched the speed of this collective advance.
Trade brought together
the creativity of thousands
and unlocked a new continent of possibilities
for adventurous seafarers.

In today's world,
with all cultures linked together by trading networks,
inventions from any place on the planet
become universal achievements of humanity.
Challenges, such as a virulent virus,
can be met with the intelligence and resources
of cultures all over the Earth's surface.
This is the noosphere in action.

Yes, the trials we face are increasing in difficulty.
But our capacity to respond collectively
is also growing.
With our digital media,
we can trade ideas instantaneously.
Humanity is becoming
a single, vast, erudite mind
at work for the potential benefit
of the entire Earth community.

7

A Brain of Brains

Over the last five hundred million years of animal evolution,
Earth's life has constructed ever more powerful brains.
This complexification process,
called cerebralization,[26]
has led to a major event
of brain-building in our time,
the construction of a global brain,
the noosphere.

More than half a billion years ago,
the first brain appeared
in a now-extinct marine animal
resembling present-day spiders and scorpions.[27]
With a nervous system
to coordinate its cells,
these early animals spread out,
and soon, there were brains
in every biome of Earth.

Life's next move was to build collective nervous systems,
such as sea jellies and coral reefs,[28]
as well as collective brains
made up of individual brains,
such as those found in ant colonies and beehives.
These collectives enjoy a greater awareness of the world
than is possible for any single individual.
Each red wood ant in a colony
knows the pathway to certain food-bearing trees.
No individual ant knows all the pathways,
but with a collective mind, the ant colony does.

Vertebrate brains engage in a similar process,
with birds forming flocks
and wolves hunting in packs.
Whereas an individual brain
can organize the cells of a wolf body,
the collective mind of a wolf pack
can organize two dozen wolves
to function as a single individual.

This movement of brain-building reached a new level
when humans constructed new collectives—
hunting groups, villages, cities—
that organized, at first, a couple of dozen individuals,
and then, in time, several hundred,
and later still, a million or more humans.
Such collectives, with their intelligence,
are new in the mammalian world.
The increase in knowledge
made possible by a million cooperating brains
has led to humanity's stunning success
as a planetary species.

Each of our nations
is a collective mind,
a brain of brains.
Members of each country
identify themselves
as "Brazilian," "American," or "Chinese."
These emotional and political identities
arise from hearing the story
of their nation's origins and development
throughout their lives.
Narrative enables
these large groups of humans
to live together
with shared meaning and purpose.

These collectives will continue,
but they have begun to recognize
they are each a smaller unit
of a larger community now forming.[29]

The narrative that reinforces this new collective
is the third story of the universe,[30]
the story of the origin and development of the universe
from the primordial flaring forth
to the emergence of millions of species of life on Earth.

Inside this global story,
we come to know ourselves
as cosmological beings.
Primarily, we are members of the Earth community.
Only secondarily are we "Brazilian," "American," or "Chinese."
As we take in this third story,
we are building a brain
of eight billion human brains,
a collective intelligence
capable of profound success
in meeting the planetary challenges
of our time.

8 | The Great Reversal

Humanity has reversed
the principal power of evolution
from diversification to convergence.
Nothing like this has happened
in the three-and-a-half billion years of life
preceding the emergence of humanity.

Diversification and convergence
are the two fundamental dynamics
of life's development.
Consider a bird species
that has found its way to a new island.
Its survival depends upon its ability
to adapt to the island's life.
It needs to learn
the bark patterns of trees,
the hunting habits of predators,
and to change its body
to correlate with these patterns.
Each change is small,
perhaps a slightly elongated beak,
but over time, the changes accumulate
and lead to new species.[31]

Because of this force of diversification,
a shrew, two hundred million years ago,
fanned out and eventually evolved
into camels, bats, elephants, and dolphins,
all from a mammal so small
it would fit in the palm of your hand.[32]

From our birthplace
two million years ago in Africa,
humans, too, diversified
into different human species:
Homo erectus,
Homo rudolfensis,
Homo soloensis,
Home sapiens,
and *Homo floresiensis*
are a few examples
of humans fanning out
into distinct species.[33]
The explosive power of differentiation
reached an endpoint, though,
with just one human species,
Homo sapiens.

We can see this shift
from diversification to convergence
in humanity's epochal journey out of Africa.
Leaving Africa,
one population went east,
another west.

The descendants of both groups met in Hawai'i,
the eastward journey completed by ancestors
of Supreme Monarch Kalani'ōpu'u,
the westward by Captain Cook.[34]
None of their ancestors
had been in contact
for hundreds of thousands of years,
yet when they encountered one another anew,
they were still the same species, *Homo sapiens*.

In their respective journeys,
each group was required
to adapt to many new biomes.
But instead of changing
their biological anatomy,
they invented specialized tools
to help them survive.
Diversification had shifted
beyond the human body
to the noospheric realm
of tools and technology.

The spread of humanity
over the entirety of Earth's surface
involved a great deal of strife.
Thousands of animal species,
including all the other human species,
suffered extinction.

We live now in a different world.
In our circumambulation, we constructed a habitat
that enveloped continents and oceans.
The powerful collective mind of *Homo sapiens*
has drawn every biome into its orbit.
The whole system of life
is now coevolving
with the noosphere of humanity.

Questions arise concerning this vast transformation.
Ultimately, will it become a beneficent change?
Will it be, instead, a tragic degradation?

We have one important clue.
The early universe began
with a rapid expansion,
the power of diversification.
After a time,
small subsets of the universe
reversed this expansion,
drew together,
and converged into stars and galaxies.

We have every reason to hope
something similar is taking place in our time.
After diversifying for three billion years,
life has reversed directions.
We can only wonder:
Though we live in a time
of widespread violence and chaos,
is this not also the birth
of a vast and majestic new era of Earth?

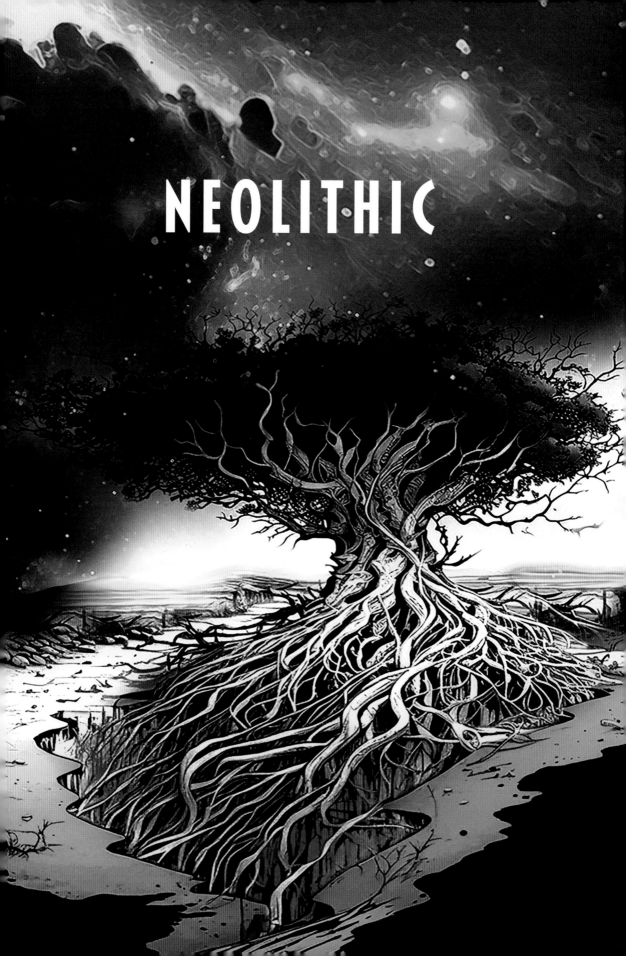

NEOLITHIC

1 NEOLITHIC HEREDITY
Sex and Soil

The Neolithic Era began
when humans discovered
the depths of future potency
in seed and topsoil,
one of the most spectacular insights
of the entire human journey.[35]

Seed and topsoil existed
for four hundred million years[36]
before their magical patterns
flickered in the mind
of one particular human genius,
a person who held in her hand
a little puff of matter,
lighter than a feather,
and realized it could bring forth
bushes and forests
and an abundance of food
never before imagined.
We have lost the name of this genius,
but not her insight.

By the power of cultural heredity—
the passage of knowledge through generations—
her discovery transformed human history.

Once our ancestral humans
knew this miracle of life,
they constructed stories
to convey their insight
to future generations.
One such story celebrated
the Mesopotamian goddess Inanna
whose numinous power suffused all life.[37]
Inanna's womb was identified with topsoil,
her lover's semen, the seeds.
Rain was understood
as the sexual act
of pressing seeds
into the generative ground.
In their annual rituals,
the king processed to the temple,
as the woman who incarnated Inanna cried out:

My vulva,
the boat of heaven,
is full of eagerness.
My untilled land lies fallow.
As for me, who art Inanna,
who will plow my vulva?
Who will plow my high field?[38]

The cultural process
of conveying wisdom
to future generations
has led to the noosphere,
a sphere of collective intelligence.
By the power of heredity,
our collective intelligence
grows stronger with every generation.
Science's ongoing investigations
have revealed the details
of soil's fecundity
which relies upon the billions of microorganisms
found in each cubic centimeter.[39]
Like the ancient Mesopotamians,
we know that by regenerating soil's vitality,
we empower all life
and all consciousness
to blossom forth.

There are perhaps one hundred billion planets
in our galaxy.
Of these, an estimated three hundred million
are Earth-like planets
that could be alive.[40]
In our Third Story understanding,
the dynamics of the Milky Way galaxy
can be understood
as a kind of cosmic topsoil
with Earth-like planets
as seeds.
Many of these seeds have birthed oceans.
Some of them might have developed life.
And one of them, without question,
is well on its way
to developing a planetary mind,
a noosphere.

2 Telling Time with Stonehenge

Thousands of years ago,
our ancestors built structures
using huge stones they had dragged
a hundred miles.[41]
This was all done by hand,
pushing boulders up and down hills,
through woodlands, across deserts.
Why?
Why push twenty-five-ton stones
a hundred miles
just to arrange them in a circle?
No one knows the whole story.
The stones do not speak.
All we can say with certainty
is that these constructions
were of immense importance
to those who built them.

Consider the structure
at Stonehenge, England.
Archaeologists are confident
it was built to celebrate
a discovery concerning
the great mystery of time.

To get a sense
of their amazing insight,
imagine what it must have been like
to live back then.
We need to keep in mind
that theirs was a time
before mechanical clocks.
No one wore a watch.
There were no cell phones.
You couldn't walk up to someone
and ask what time it was,
expecting to hear
something like "9:30."

These Neolithic humans
discovered a pattern in time
that came not from humans
but from the universe itself.

To understand what they discovered,
imagine being with them
in the forests of southern England.
They would explain to us
that the sun rises each morning
at a different spot on the horizon.
Day by day, the sun would be seen
to move a tiny bit to the south.
But then, something amazing would happen.
A day would come
when the sun stopped moving.
The next day, an equally amazing event
would take place.
The sun would move in the other direction,
and with each new dawn,
the sun would appear on the horizon
a tiny bit to the north.

This discovery took place
on every continent.
Stonehenge in Europe,
Chichén Itzá in Mesoamerica,
New Grange in Ireland[42]—
all were constructed
to amplify our awareness
of the day when the sun stands still.

On that special day
in the mound at New Grange,
light penetrates into the structure
and lights up an interior
that is dark every other day.
Do you see what this means?
Our ancestors had discovered
a pattern in time—the year.
A stellar action in the cosmos
had come to an end
and now would start a new year.
Days would grow longer
and the whole cycle
would happen again.
Our ancestors were learning
to place themselves
inside the ritual
of the Sun and other stars.[43]
Something of supreme importance
had been discovered,
and they knew it.

To celebrate this revelation
they dragged boulders a hundred miles
and built structures
weighing five million tons.
They created these architectural wonders
to embed a sacred pattern of time
into human awareness.

A similar event
is taking place today.
Over the thousands of years that separate us
from the construction of Stonehenge,
we've developed new tools
for beholding the universe:
telescopes, Geiger counters,
mathematics, computers.
With these powers of perception,
we have discovered
a new dimension of time.
Whereas Neolithic humans
saw the movement
of the sun through the year,
we contemporary humans
have discovered a new kind of movement:
the movement of the universe
through its development.
We now know the universe
has undergone two strong transformations.[44]
First, the primal light became the galaxies,
and second,
the stellar systems gave birth to life.
Our time now
is the third transformation,
the appearance on Earth
of planetary mind,
a unified humanity.

Our ancestors built stone temples
to celebrate their discovery.
We follow their example,
building a new kind of Stonehenge.
This book and other works of art
are designed to place
the sacred pattern of developmental time
into human awareness.[45]
Just as Stonehenge showed humans
that winter solstice came on one day,
and one day only,
so too, the chapters of this book
celebrate a new, cosmic, evolutionary sense of time—
our time now, the one and only time
when the noosphere emerges.[46]

3

Cave Art and Symbolic Imagination

Over the last million years,
the human mind has been assembled
through a series of awakenings,
the most powerful of which
was symbolic imagination.[47]
Coming to understand
the evocation of symbolic imagination
will help us recognize something similar
taking place in our time.

The early form of symbolic imagination
was an enhancement of memory.
We need to keep in mind
that memory itself
is an activity of the entire cosmos.
Everything you see—
the stars, the sky,
the forest, your hometown,
your family, your body—
draws upon memory for its existence.
Memory is something matter does,
even in its most rudimentary forms.[48]

For instance, consider the craters on the moon.
These craters remain the same,
century after century.
Their physical forms
hold the effects of impacts
that took place millions of years ago.
The shape of each crater
is the way matter remembers
those specific events.

With life, we find a new form of memory.
With every breath we take,
we create energy
using the protein molecule cytochrome c.[49]
Cytochrome c was first created
billions of years ago,
and life learned to remember
how to build it,
generation after generation.

With more advanced animals,
life developed a form of memory
enabling complicated journeys.
The red knot sandpiper
remembers how to fly
from the southern tip of South America
to the Arctic each spring.
There are no neon signs
telling the bird where to turn.
The red knot's memory
enables it to navigate
this nine-thousand-mile flight.[50]

A hundred thousand years ago,
humans developed
yet another form of memory,
that of symbolic imagination.
This new ability
allowed humans to dwell
on a past experience
in the present moment.
This deepened and complexified
the human mind.

Let's consider one of the places
where symbolic imagination first emerged.
Imagine we are Cro-Magnon humans
entering Rouffignac cave in southern France
thousands of years ago.[51]
We would crawl on our backs
a half-mile into Earth's depths.
Imagine being there,
our torchlights flickering on the walls.
In the darkness,
we would draw straight and curvy lines
on a rock wall.

We use the phrase "straight and curvy lines"
to emphasize the strangeness of this event.
Why did we descend
half a mile into the Earth?
It was not for food or sexual mates.
We went for the strange experience
of gazing at a rock wall
with squiggly lines
that suddenly became a galloping horse.
These lines,
made of charcoal mixed with saliva,
enabled us to imagine a horse,
even though no horse
was physically present.
Our ancestors crawled into caves
for sixty thousand years
because of the exhilarating experience
of presencing more of the universe through art.
Only because they evoked
the power of symbolic imagination
can we now say,
thousands of years later,
"Imagine we are Cro-Magnon humans
entering into Rouffignac cave."

Humans today are bringing forth planetary mind,
a new dimension of consciousness,
one as significant as symbolic imagination.
As planetary mind,
we experience not only the world at hand,
but by enhancing our senses
with telescopes, sonar, and x-rays,
we experience the universe
in its vast complexity.[52]
Not only are we in touch
with those who are close by,
we have also found our way
into planetary connections
far beyond our local space and time.

The experience currently emerging,
where the individual consciously contributes
to the awakening of the noosphere,
might be disorienting.
It will take time.
But we will learn to participate
in this new cosmic power
just as we learned
to navigate symbolic imagination.

Our aim in these chapters
is to explore
the nature of the noospheric mind,
understanding it
in order to collaborate with it.
Each of us has a role to play.
Working together,
we will bring forth
a new era of flourishing
for the entire Earth community
and beyond.

4 Singing the Universe into Being

Humans today have a collective challenge:
the invention of pathways
into deeper, more harmonious communities.

As we undertake this challenge,
it is helpful to remember
that the construction of communities
is one of three principal aims of the universe
from the beginning of time.[53]
It happens at every level.
Scattered atoms are brought together
in the community of a star.
Immense numbers of stars are drawn together
in the community of a galaxy.
On Earth, individual cells are woven
into the multicellular community
of a tree or an animal.

This process continues with groups.
Wolves construct packs,
birds gather into flocks,
and chimpanzees assemble themselves in troops.

Hundreds of thousands of years ago,
humans emerged inside this cosmological process.
One of the most potent artistic techniques
invented for the building of community
was the ritual.

To get a sense of ritual's power,
consider the Kalapalo in central Brazil,
a tribe that did not encounter modern civilization
until late in the nineteenth century.[54]

The Kalapalo live in two worlds.
For three seasons—fall, winter, and spring—
they organize their society
at the level of kin groups.
During the summer season, however,
they give themselves over to rituals
that perform their cosmology.
In ritual, they aim to meld
with powerful beings
from the beginning of time.

In their understanding,
the ritual itself gives birth
to these powerful beings.
The ritual sings them into existence.
As the singing and dancing continues
for weeks and even months,
there is a merging of the singers
with the entities they are singing about.

In the joy of this collective experience,
they transcend their smaller, familial identities.
In the deep experience of the ritual,
they can say:
"I am the Kalapalo people,"
and not only,
"I am Kambe's daughter-in-law."

To say, "I am the Kalapalo people,"
is to awaken to a larger dimension of self.
For the Kalapalo,
ritual enabled the participants
to create a deeper community.

Today, there is perhaps no more significant challenge
than the invention of processes
that will enable contemporary humans
all around our planet
to do something similar,
to move from the fragmentation
of our nation-states
to the unity of our Earth community,
and to feel in a primary way
that we are Earth,
we are universe,
first and foremost.
Everything else is secondary.

We need new rituals
set in the context
of contemporary cosmology,
rituals that sing of a cosmic birth
fourteen billion years ago,
that developed into stars,
galaxies, living planets,
and human reflective consciousness.

The powerful being
we sing into existence
is that of the noosphere,
a unified humanity.
Immersed in artistic rituals
within the context of a developing humanity
within an evolving universe,
our experience will lead us to say,
"I am part of collective humanity,"
and not only,
"I am American," or "I am Chinese."
Together, we create
a song that evokes
a flourishing Earth community.

5 The Cosmic Law of Love

The power of attraction
is a foundational dynamic of development,
present throughout the history of the universe.
Even at the level of gravity and chemistry,
atoms, attracted to one another,
give birth to stars and planets,
while elements, drawn to bond together,
enable the emergence of life.
On the human level,
attraction might have different names—
fascination, allurement, love—
but the dynamism is the same:
when two or more entities
are drawn into union,
new and vital potencies for creativity manifest.
We call this the "Cosmic Law of Love"
because it holds
at every level of development
and throughout all time.[55]

This power that emerges with union
holds at the collective level as well.
We see the cosmic law of love at work
in the explosion of creativity
that characterized humanity's crossover
to the Neolithic Era.
For a hundred thousand years,
humanity had lived in small groups
of a couple of dozen people.
As disparate bands of humans
entered into union
and population centers grew into the thousands,
new approaches to the perennial challenges
of growing food and raising families
were invented.
We created pottery.
We invented a new substance, concrete,
and constructed buildings
that would last for centuries.[56]
We made proto-writing inscriptions
on clay tablets.[57]

All of this creativity arose
From our deepening bonds
with one another.
By pursuing the fascinations
that emerged in village communities,
humanity created entirely new modes
of being human.

Fourteen billion years ago,
the matter of the universe
consisted of vast clouds of hydrogen.
Try a thought experiment:
Imagine you are a hydrogen atom
near a cloud of atoms
whose population is near
the crossover point
for becoming a star.[58]
You, of course, have no idea
that by joining this cloud,
you will make the gravitational attraction
large enough to begin fusing
hydrogen into helium.
But your addition will, in fact,
transform this cloud
from random motion
to the self-organizing dynamism
of a star.

With respect to the noosphere,
we are at a similar crossover point.

In our global village,
with its instantaneous communication systems,
the myriad possibilities
for creative union among humans
have exploded
from two dozen in the Paleolithic Era
to substantially more today.
A kaleidoscope of differentiation
is coming forth
as we pursue these new possibilities.

Are you interested in learning music
from African drummers?
With a flick of your finger,
you can begin.
What about the principles of robotics
from world experts at Stanford University?
Your teachers are eager
for your online participation.
Why not become a journalist
with one of history's most celebrated sportswriters?
All of these, and a billion more avenues for development,
are offered to you by the noosphere.

Though its full reality is yet to appear,
the noosphere is already at work.
It does not speak English or Chinese.
It conveys its wisdom
in the language of longing,
of desire, of beauty.

Allow fascination to lead the way.
To find the courage,
bear in mind, always,
that something as significant
as a star is emerging.
Something as amazing
as a living cell is bursting forth.
Each of us is given the opportunity
to become a person
who could not have come forth
in previous eras of human history.
By becoming the person
we are destined to be,
we enable the noosphere
to rise.

6 Obsidian and Circulatory Networks

With the emergence of humans,
a new form of trade
involving reflective consciousness
was initiated on planet Earth.
By examining the power of trading networks,
we get a clear view
of how they led
to greater intelligence and deeper harmony
throughout humanity.

To see this transformative power in action,
let's examine the Neolithic trade networks
of a single, rare material, obsidian.

Obsidian is a unique form of glass
made by volcanoes.
In Neolithic Mexico,
it was highly valued
as an excellent material
for making arrowheads.
But there was one difficulty.
Since obsidian is found only near volcanoes,
if you happened to live elsewhere,
you were forced either to steal it
or to wage war
with the people
who possessed it.

Neolithic humans conceived a new approach.
They paid attention to the "others,"
the enemies who hoarded obsidian.
They learned about their hardships and privations,
and took on the challenge
of satisfying their various desires.
They learned to harvest honey,
constructed beautiful ceramic pots,[59]
and offered these goods
in exchange for obsidian.
Their empathetic actions
led to mutual enhancement.
Because of their deepening relationships,
each group was more prosperous.
Each thrived in new ways
because of trade.

In this sense, trade is a human form
of the co-evolutionary dynamic at work
in the lifeworld
and throughout the universe
from the beginning.
Consider this dynamic at play
between the hawk and the mouse.[60]
The mouse, required to contend with the hawk,
develops, over many generations,
a keener sensitivity
to a predator's attack.
It works in the opposite direction as well.
The hawk's difficulty
in dealing with the speed of the mouse
leads to sharper eyesight
and more effective cognition
in the hawk's offspring.
Out of these tense relationships,
both species thrive.

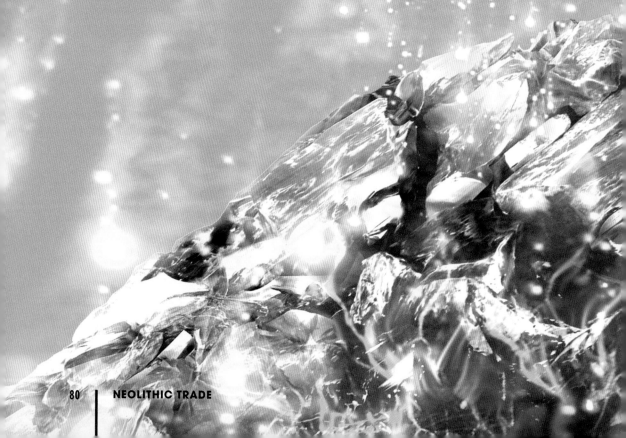

If we rise to places
high above the plateau
of Neolithic Mexico,
we can see
these co-evolutionary trade networks
constitute a circulatory system.
In this dynamic system,
essential elements for human development,
such as obsidian,
flow from areas of high concentration
to places that lack these elements.[61]
Entire regions come to life
when potent elements are distributed
throughout networks of trade.

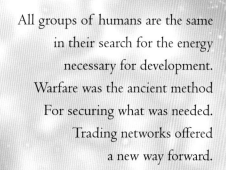

All groups of humans are the same
in their search for the energy
necessary for development.
Warfare was the ancient method
For securing what was needed.
Trading networks offered
a new way forward.

Through face-to-face intimacy,
we come to feel
what the other deeply desires.
As we create
the mutually enhancing interactions of trade,
we transform so-called "others"
into partners with whom we thrive.

NEOLITHIC CEREBRALIZATION
Steps toward a Planetary Intelligence

Throughout three billion years of life,
the mysterious power of intelligence
deepened and spread.

We live amid a new irruption,
an emergence vast,
a mind planetary.
The noosphere is coming alive.

What is intelligence
but the capacity to figure things out?[62]
When our ancestors invented the spear,
our creative intelligence
extended beyond the biological body
into wood and stone.[63]

Then, ten thousand years ago,
humans discovered
the collective mind of gregarious herds.
In so doing, they extended their own minds
into the relationships of other collective entities.

They lured bison to an unseen cliff,[64]
raised a great noise and charged from the rear.
A human decoy wearing a bison skin
emerged from hiding and sprinted toward the cliff.
The bison, deceived, charged past the decoy,
and with hooves still churning through thin air,
plummeted to a group death.

The action of these Neolithic humans
reflects an understanding of relationships
at work in the herd.
Participation in planetary intelligence
deepened when our ancestors
began domesticating animals
such as turkeys and wolves.[65]
By restricting sexual reproduction
to those animals possessing traits desirable to us,
we shaped bodies not yet born.
With plants, this led to potatoes, squash, and corn.
The mind of humanity
had moved into the future
of animal bodies and cultivated fields
that would one day envelop Earth.

Breakthroughs in planetary intelligence
continue today
as humanity comes to understand
the mind of Earth itself.

Over the past four billion years,
the Sun's core temperature
has soared a million degrees.[66]
And yet,
Earth's life has survived.
If Earth had been passive,
the increasing temperature of the Sun
would have eliminated life.
But Earth is not a passive receiver
of the Sun's energy.
The collective Earth system
has altered atmospheres and oceans
in ways that have protected life.

We live not on the surface of Earth.
We live inside its mind.
We are this mind
becoming aware of itself.

The challenge
is to realize our destiny.
To carry planetary intelligence further.
To feel our way
into a flourishing future.
To remember that we live inside Earth's mind.
And to take in this mind-blowing fact:
the future of our planet
passes through the consciousness
of a single species.[67]
We are that species.
Humanity is the reflective self-awareness
of the solar system.

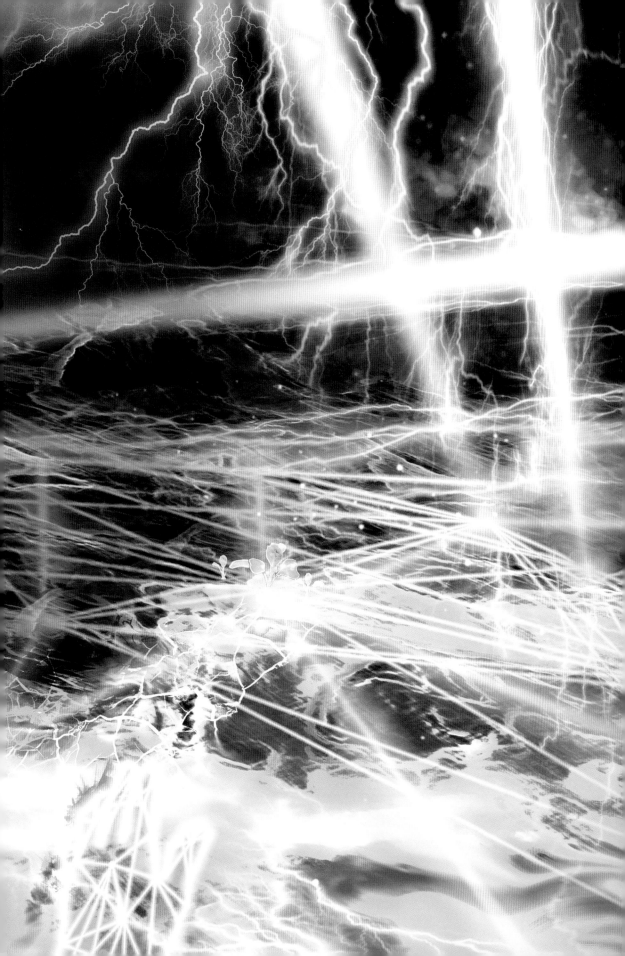

8

Synergy and Creative Relationships

One of the most creative forces
in the universe is synergy.[68]
Through synergy,
relationships give birth to powers that only exist
in the union of two or more entities.
Synergistic potencies are present
at all levels of the universe,
from the primordial plasma
to the depths of human relationships.

Consider the elementary particles of the universe:
protons, neutrons, and electrons.
Whereas protons and electrons are stable,
neutrons have a lifetime of just a few minutes.
A free-floating neutron
will exist for fifteen minutes,
then split apart.[69]

But if you combine a neutron with a proton,
the neutron will not decay.
Neutrons together with protons
survive for billions of years.
The synergistic transformation of the neutron
into a stable member of an atom
is the foundation of all physical structure.[70]

The creative power of synergy is evident
when geological processes of Earth
are contrasted with those of the moon.
Twentieth-century space exploration
provides empirical evidence
that the mineral composition
of moon and Earth surfaces
are almost identical.[71]
The difference, then,
between the lifeless moon
and the living Earth
comes from the mixing of substances
that took place on Earth,
which led to millions of chemical relationships
among the different elements,
some of which eventuated in the living cell.
The moon froze early in its existence,
and without the capacity
to bring different elements into contact,
the synergy of chemical combinations
could not be explored.

One last example of synergy's power
is the eukaryotic cell.
Though smaller than the eye can see,
the eukaryotic diatoms, taken together,
produce close to half of the atmosphere's oxygen,
This alone is an impressive achievement,[72]
but consider this additional fact:
If a hundred billion eukaryotic cells
are knitted together
in a very particular way,
we have the human brain.
The functioning of the oceanic eukaryote, the diatom,
is substantially the same
as the functioning of each eukaryotic brain cell.
In synergistic relationship,
a collection of eukaryotic cells
is transformed into something radically new:
a network that creates symphonic music,
scientific theory, and complex civilizations.
The human mind arises
From the synergistic relations
of its constituent cells.
Such is the magic of synergy—
it produces its benefits as if pulling them out of thin air.

So now, let's ask the most fundamental question.
How do we participate in the power of synergy?
Our relationships determine
our achievements in life.
The challenge is to find others
who share our fundamental aspirations.
When we enter into relationship with them,
all of us become more creative.

When we find a special person,
or a special group of persons,
our relationships bring forth
a power of creativity
that manifests and deepens
as long as we remain connected.
With the emergence of the noosphere,
a new level of creative power is at hand.
Relationships at the planetary level
enable us to work together as a species
toward a flourishing Earth community.
Through deepening relationships
that enhance technologies of communication,
expand global trade,
and evoke new forms of consciousness,
the noosphere is rising.

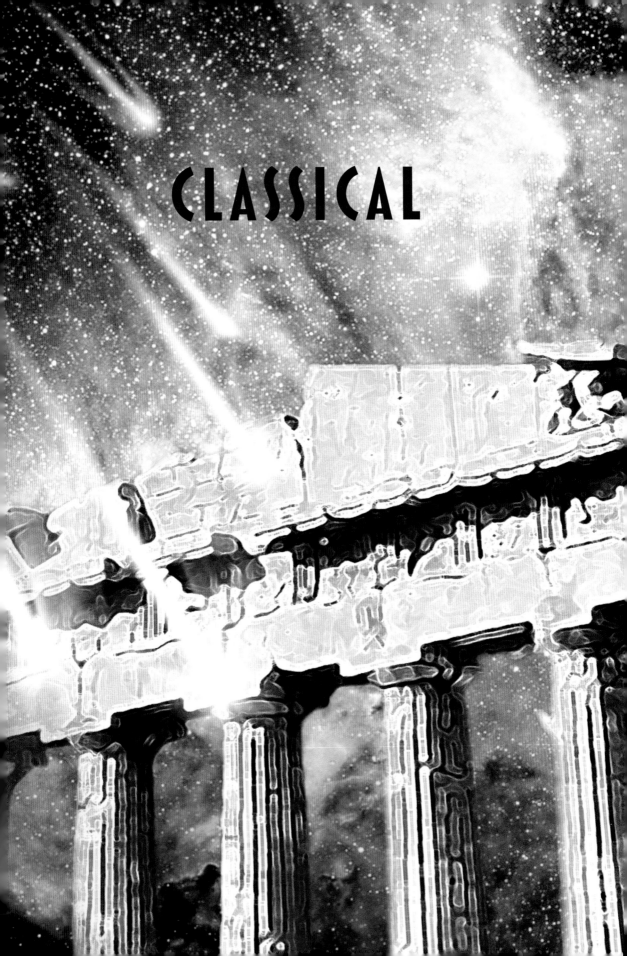

CLASSICAL

1 CLASSICAL HEREDITY
The Universe Is Thinking

Civilization began
when we noticed for the first time
we were thinking.

Humans had been thinking for millions of years.
In our journeys out of Africa,
we thought about the many things we encountered,
things we had never seen before—
snowfall,
the Pacific Ocean,
woolly mammoths.

But after exploring all of Earth's continents,
we noticed something
none of our ancestors had mentioned.
We noticed we were aware.
We noticed we were thinking.
Something new was taking place.
Instead of thinking about this or that thing,
we were thinking about thinking.
For the first time in the history of humanity,
thought itself became an object of thought.[73]

In ancient Greek civilization,
the capacity to think
was named "soul."
Soul is a treasure passed down to us,
a treasure we are still developing.

The soul is bottomless in its reflections.
When one thinks, who is thinking?[74]
Where is the origin of one's thoughts?
What is one's ground?
Is it the soul within one's body that is thinking?

Imagine a mother and her toddler
walking on a forest trail
when suddenly,
a wolf leaps out of the woods.
Filled with fright, the mother charges.
Who is it that is charging the wolf?
Where does her courage come from?

Two hundred fifty million years
of violent predator attacks
shape the intense bond
between a mammalian mother and her babies.
When the mother leaps to protect her child,
her body correlates
with untold generations preceding her.

The entire entangled complex
of relationships going back millions of years
is called the "hyperbody."[75]
Every mammal has a visible body
inside a vast, invisible hyperbody
that includes a cosmic memory
of incalculable mother-child bonds.

Our bodies, woven into time,
reach out to the full history of the universe.
Both the body and the hyperbody
are the source of our decisions.

Twenty-five hundred years ago,
humans were stunned to realize
they had the power of thinking.
Something of equal significance
is taking place presently.
We realize that when we think,
it is the universe thinking as us.
As we come to realize
the universe is alive within us,[76]
Earth becomes ever more deeply
a thinking planet.

2 Pyramids and Flying Insects

One of the persistent challenges for humanity
is maintaining our zest for life.
This is especially true
in the early twenty-first century
when chaos and confusion reign.
To avoid cynicism and despair,
it is vital we perceive
a deeper meaning to the chaos
and come to understand our power
in relation to the whole of things.[77]
We step beyond nihilism
and access deep wellsprings of psychic energy
when we feel, even momentarily,
that we are a part
of an epochal transformation.

Homo sapiens have existed for 300,000 years.[78]
For most of that time,
we received food from Earth
just as children are fed by their parents.
Trees provided nuts,
forests provided root vegetables,
migrating herds of animals
provided meat.
Throughout all of this,
humans adapted
to the complex ecologies of their place.
Then the vast transformation began.
Human minds, burning with a desire to know,
deepened our understanding of the natural world
and created tools
that magnified our collective power.

Suddenly, we found ourselves
creating the Great Wall of China,
the psychedelic Madurai Meenakshi Amman temple in India,
and the Pyramid of the Sun in Mexico.
Life had never seen such structures
over its three-and-a-half billion years of evolution.

These architectonic constructions
were the first moments
when humans realized
they possessed planet-sized powers.
What did it mean that we could build such things?
What is the purpose of this stupendous power?

To reflect on these profound questions,
consider a homologous moment
in life's evolution.

Millions of years ago,
insects grew lobe fans on their backs
to regulate their temperature.
This adaptation enabled them
to survive throughout the planet.
Then, a surprise took place.
The lobe fans had become large enough
to lift them off the ground.
Insects were moving
with the power of the wind
for the first time in the history of the animal world.[79]
One can imagine
there must have been some initial confusion.
The DNA of these insects
had come from living on flat land.
Now, the two-dimensional minds of the insects
had to navigate three-dimensional space.
After a learning period, they figured it out.
The insects became pollinators for trees.
They co-evolved with flowers and rivers
throughout the continents.
Nothing like this had happened before.
The flying insects gave birth
to a new life world.

It is the same with us.
We have been confused
by our technological power
and have made catastrophic mistakes,
such as the Dust Bowl in America,
which destroyed soil communities
built up over a hundred thousand years.[80]
Just like the insects,
we are being transformed by our technologies
and are now learning
to manage our planet-sized power.

Those of us alive today
find ourselves at the brink
of a new era of thriving life,
engendered by processes
that are driving self-organization
to the crossing of a new threshold,
the noosphere.[81]
The way ahead is to imagine and reach,
energized by the creativity
that flows from the experience
of zest and fascination
and from alignment
with deep processes of the universe
already underway.

Zarathustra and the New Leap in Being

3

For thousands of years,
whenever humans spoke of profound matters,
we were quoting the words of the gods.
Athena, the Olympian Goddess, said "this,"
or Ra, the Egyptian Sun God, said "that."
Such statements from sacred scriptures
were regarded as eternal, unalterable, and perfect.
What mattered for the order of society
was obedience to these pronouncements.[82]

Then, a man came forward.
He had a way of talking
that changed the world forever.
His name was Zarathustra.
He was one of history's earliest individuals
to express an internal sense of self-consciousness.
Because of him,
each of us now has a unique identity.

In this chapter, we examine
the Zarathustrian transformation
into self-consciousness
so that we might better understand
our opportunity today
for a new transformation of consciousness.

Zarathustra was born in present-day Iran
sometime during the second millennium
before the Common Era.
We have little biographical knowledge of him
beyond the poems he wrote,
the seventeen Gathas.
Only six thousand words altogether,
they were enough to cause
a revolution in consciousness.
Instead of being yet another collection
of divine utterances,
Zarathustra's poems were a dialogue
between himself and his Supreme God,
Ahura Mazda.
This was his radical act:
He conceived of himself
as being an active participant.

In the Ushtavaiti Gatha,
he tells of his first meeting:

"I realize Thou art prosperous,
O wise Ahura Mazda,
who asks me, 'Who art thou?'
I say . . . 'I am Zarathustra.'"[83]

"I am Zarathustra"
is one of history's earliest written expressions
of self-consciousness.
Zarathustra was aware,
and he was aware of himself as being aware.

Self-consciousness was emerging
in others of his era as well,
including the priestess, Enheduanna,
and the lawgiver, Hammurabi.
But it was Zarathustra
who invented a method
for awakening self-consciousness in others.
He instructed people to examine themselves
on a daily basis,
to reflect upon their thoughts,
their words,
and their actions,
and to ask themselves
the simple question:
"Am I on the side of truth?
Or falsehood?"

By getting people to turn their attention
back upon themselves,
he brought forth the form of consciousness
we now call a conscience.
Through the practice of introspection,
humans deepened their awareness.
They were no longer part
of the undifferentiated assemblage
of a despotic ruler,
but became, over time,
active, responsible human agents.
This development can be called
a "leap in being."[84]

Our own moment
includes the possibility
for a leap in being
of comparable significance.[85]
Four and a half centuries of modern science
have led to the discovery
of the evolutionary nature
of the universe.
Now, when we turn our attention
back on ourselves,
we come to realize
we are not only moral, responsible agents,
we are, in fact,
the latest development
of the universe itself.

Our bodies have been assembled
by fourteen billion years of creativity.
Our minds have been developed
by three hundred thousand years
of human consciousness.
By reflecting on this new understanding,
which is what you are doing
when you engage with this book,
you become aware
that the universe, as a whole,
is an active agent.
That the universe, as a whole,
is acting in the form of you.
The question in our time concerns alignment.
Are our thoughts, words, and actions
aligned with the Earth's primary aim?
To bring forth a unified humanity?

CLASSICAL COMMUNICATION

4 | Written Language and the Mind of Humanity

Beginning six thousand years ago,
humans discovered written language,
a new form of communication
that enhanced the ongoing construction
of the mind of humanity.

Archaeologists speculate it was our desire
to keep track of economic transactions
that led to the invention
of making marks on clay.[86]
Holding the details of trade negotiations
in one human mind
had proven impossible.
Crucial facts had been misremembered.
Arguments and fights had erupted.
But with the invention of written language,
important agreements made in the past
were recorded onto objects
that lasted through time.

Once symbols for financial arrangements were established,
humans began storing
other aspects of their experience
in marks on clay.
Traditions of literature, poetry, and philosophy
came forth all around the planet.[87]
Rare insights into the meaning of existence
were stowed in cultural objects
and carried to others in far-off lands,
even to those in future generations.
This was altogether new.
Written language enabled past achievements
of thought and action
to be communicated to the present.

The universe, from the beginning,
has struggled to preserve its accomplishments.
Consider a group of photons
landing on Earth's surface.
If they collide with a rock,
some will be reflected back into space,
while others will be transformed
into a small puff of warmth.
But should these photons land on a leaf,
they will be captured by the chlorophylls
and stowed in energetic molecules.
Trees did not invent the first photosynthetic molecules.
That invention took place
billions of years before trees evolved.[88]
DNA molecules captured the invention
and passed it on,
generation to generation,
to contemporary trees.
DNA enables life's great accomplishments
to be present now
so that contemporary plants and animals
can build on them.

Something similar takes place with the noosphere.
With the invention of written language,
the deepest insights into wisdom
could be captured and held in libraries.
Henceforth, whenever new human beings
wondered over the meaning of their existence,
they could join an ancient lineage.
Each new quest for wisdom
could begin with the most advanced thoughts
of the most brilliant humans
in all of history.

In this sense, we can say
that life created the genetic code
to awaken the vitality of animals,
whereas civilizations created literature
to awaken the mind and heart
of humanity.

When we today
engage with books, art, music,
the power of language
enables us to commune
with the creators,
to shape their frozen energies
into new meaning.
Their feelings, ideas,
emotions, and insights
have been preserved by the noosphere
to ignite our latent creativity.
In our search for wisdom,
we start from where they left off.
And when the light comes on,
when we are suddenly burning with conviction
about how to move forward with our lives,
we can also feel
that it was the noosphere
that lit this passion
and that we
have become the noosphere.
We are living at the front.[89]
We are fourteen billion years
burst into awareness of itself.

5

The Extraordinary Realm

As humans deepened their relationships,
they became aware of an extraordinary realm
beyond actual people and things,
a realm with a great many names,
like Dao, Heaven,
the transcendent, paradise.[90]
The extraordinary realm
is untouchable, unseeable,
and yet, a realm of such great force,
it changed the structure of human society.

When the populations of cities grew large,
a small segment of humanity
began to dwell on questions
unrelated to the practical concerns of survival.
They began to ask,
"Why are we here?
What is our true nature?
Where are we headed?"

Their quest became formalized
when individuals joined together
in universities and temples.
Entire lives were devoted to study,
to meditation and prayer,
to philosophical reflection,
and to rational debate.

Because relationships are mutually evocative,
these privileged persons
found the extraordinary realm
beyond actual entities.
They could feel its potencies
pressing into them.[91]
By actualizing these potencies,
they were transformed
into higher and deeper
manifestations of humanity.

Words had to be invented
to identify what they had become:
sages, prophets,
rishis, scholars,
shamans, mahatmas, saints.

The cost of these breakthroughs
was borne by hundreds of thousands of serfs.
The pyramid is the central image
of the hierarchical structure
of classical civilization:
the chosen few at the pinnacle,
the rest of the population
crushed by the backbreaking work
of medieval agriculture.
A tiny segment of the population
was free to focus
on intellectual and spiritual development
while the vast majority
lived lives of drudgery.

The spiritual development
of the select few
led to a dramatic reversal.
Intuitions surfacing in the privileged
deconstructed the world
that had brought them forth.
The best minds and spirits
of classical civilization
brought about the demise
of classical civilization.
A radical equality
at the foundation of humanity
cried out for change.

Dramatic reversal is the way of the universe.

Four billion years earlier,
the dynamics of a molten Earth,
roasted by the sun's radiant energy,
cooked minerals into living cells.[92]
Proliferating exponentially,
cellular life consumed
the very conditions
that had brought it forth.

Dreams of the extraordinary realm
appeared first in a rarified few
and soon churned
within the hearts
of humans everywhere.
Had we been born three thousand years ago,
we would likely have been confined
to the narrow world of serfdom.
Today, humanity is offered
many opportunities for the development of soul,
formerly reserved for a privileged few.

Two centuries ago, the majority of humanity
lived in extreme poverty.
Out of the increased productivity
of synergistic relationships and deepening intelligence,
the number in extreme poverty today
has fallen dramatically.

You may hear this and find yourself thinking,
"Impoverishment for even one percent of society
is unacceptable."
If so, your response manifests
the reality of the extraordinary realm.
You see beyond *what is* to what *could be*.
And should you decide to dedicate your life
to the total eradication of extreme poverty,
you become convincing proof
of its powerful force.
A better world is pressing in upon us.
Our connection to this unseeable realm
is through the fascinations and allurements
that speak to us of new possibilities.
The unseeable world
we are drawn toward
is the noosphere rising.

6 CLASSICAL TRADE
Money and Wealth

Money, invented during the classical period of humanity,
drove a new era of human evolution.
Money was such a powerful force,
we are only now beginning to realize
money and wealth
are two entirely different realities.
In order to understand
how they are related,
we consider one of the first appearances of money
which occurred in the third century BCE in China.

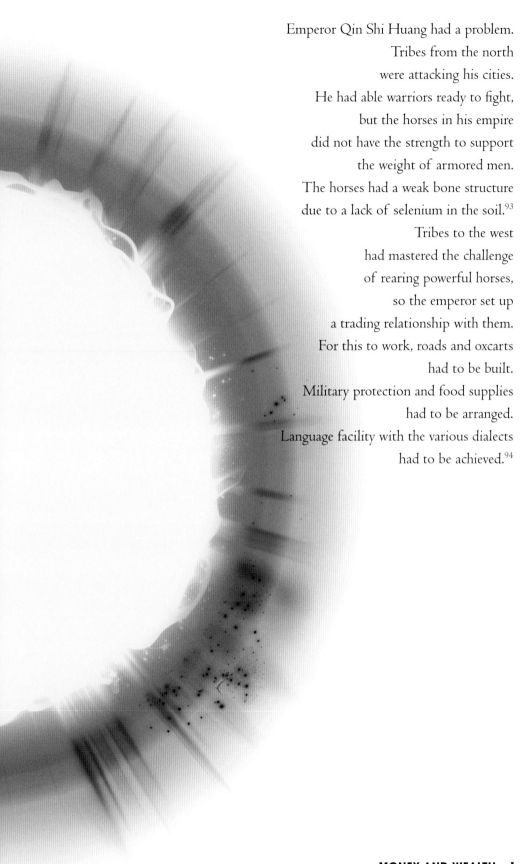

Emperor Qin Shi Huang had a problem.
Tribes from the north
were attacking his cities.
He had able warriors ready to fight,
but the horses in his empire
did not have the strength to support
the weight of armored men.
The horses had a weak bone structure
due to a lack of selenium in the soil.[93]
Tribes to the west
had mastered the challenge
of rearing powerful horses,
so the emperor set up
a trading relationship with them.
For this to work, roads and oxcarts
had to be built.
Military protection and food supplies
had to be arranged.
Language facility with the various dialects
had to be achieved.[94]

In the midst of all these complications,
the emperor envisioned
the concept of money.
In China's case, it was copper coins.[95]
With this new means of exchange,
myriad products along the entire trade route
could be converted first to coins,
and then, to whatever product was desired.
By its ability to transform
any human product
into any other human product,
money enabled trade to soar.

An entirely unexpected capacity of money
changed the course of history.
In order to understand this feature,
we turn to the universe as a whole.

The universe proceeds
by storing vast amounts of energy
in forms that can be used
for creative action.
For instance, as the universe expands,
it transforms heat into gravitational energy.

Imagine a small volume of the primordial fireball
as it expands to a sphere
trillions of miles in diameter.
The sphere is cooler
than the primordial plasma,
but the atoms now possess
enough gravitational energy
to contract violently
and create stars.[96]

The same phenomenon happens in the lifeworld.
With the invention of photosynthesis,
photons of sunlight
can be captured by the chlorophylls
and stored as energy.
In this way, the tiny puffs of energy
from individual photons are accumulated,
and, at a later time,
transformed into a cheetah
running sixty miles an hour.[97]

In the case of early China,
Qin Shi Huang amassed
a huge amount of copper coins,
enough to construct the Great Wall of China.
It is money's energy-storing capacity
that enables so much to happen.
It empowered humans
to build cathedrals and skyscrapers,
structures more colossal
than anything hitherto created
in three billion years of biological life.

No wonder humans became mesmerized by money.

But humans do not exist to accumulate money.
We exist to build wealth.

In our example of ancient China,
money consisted of copper coins
made by the emperor.
The copper coins were not wealth.
Wealth consisted of the land,
the transportation systems,
the skill to create ceramics and silk clothing,
the efficiency of monetary exchange,
the communication systems,
the keeping of records,
the protection of trade routes,
and the wisdom for rearing strong horses.
Wealth consisted of this entire system.

Money is a way of storing
the energy of human creativity,
whereas wealth is the capacity
to activate human creativity.

Building wealthy systems
is our primary aim and ultimate meaning.
When we build wealth,
we are building the noosphere.

7 | CLASSICAL CEREBRALIZATION
Pythagorean Dreams

The special nature of human consciousness
is bringing forth a planet that is ever more mind-like.
"Cerebralization" is the word we use
for the process of extending and deepening mentality.[98]

Is this work of cerebralization
coming from the universe?
Or are we on our own?
Are we a meaningless speck
in the midst of a trillion galaxies?
Or are we fulfilling the cosmic task
of constructing a planetary mind?
Such questions have gripped humans
from the beginning.

One fascinating speculation
that comes from the world of science
suggests a radical new understanding
of our existence as humans.

The breakthrough took place in southern Italy
when Pythagoras and other Greek philosophers
made the metaphysical assertion
that the cosmos is composed of numbers.
Historians surmise that this daring speculation
came from a remarkable discovery made by musicians
concerning the quality of sound their instruments created.
With respect to a Greek lyre,
its tonality depended on the ratios of the string lengths.
If the ratios were made with whole numbers,
the sound coming forth was music.
If the ratio was irrational,
only noise was produced.
The Pythagoreans leapt from this discovery
to the idea that the harmonious movements
of the stars and planets
came from their being constructed
with rational mathematical ratios.
This wild speculation,
that mathematics was the foundation of the world,
launched the investigation
we now call mathematical physics.
Our trips to the moon, our skyscrapers,
and our electronic communication technology
are all made possible
by developments of the ancient intuition
that numbers structure the universe.

This investigation continues
even two and a half millennia after Pythagoras
in the work of Paul Adrien Maurice Dirac,
the Nobel Prize–winning physicist
who founded quantum field theory.
Dirac compared the strength of electricity
to the strength of gravity
and found an extraordinarily large number:
ten raised to the fortieth power.
He then calculated
the number of elementary particles
in the entire universe
and found that same number,
ten to the fortieth, now squared.[99]
When he examined ratios of other processes,
again and again, he arrived at this same number,
which convinced him he had stumbled upon
a fundamental order of the universe.

The climax came when he considered
the age of the universe,
commonly measured at fourteen billion years.
But a year is not a universal unit of time.
If we go back in time to before there was an Earth,
the concept of "year" has no meaning.
Physicists employ a universal unit of time,
called a "jiffy," which is the time interval
required by a photon
to cross the diameter of an elementary particle.
When the age of the universe
was calculated in these universal units,
it was found, to everyone's astonishment,
that it was ten to the fortieth.

That the age of the universe
was this same number was stunning.
After all, unlike the ratio of electricity and gravity,
the age of the universe is *changing*.
Was it really just a simple accident
that Dirac happened to calculate the age
when the universal time was ten to the fortieth?

No, it was not a coincidence.
As one of Dirac's colleagues pointed out,
ten to the fortieth jiffies
is not some abstract interval of time.
It is the time when the universe
complexified enough to determine its age.
This complexification was possible
only because in every concrete event,
over billions of years,
the universe as a whole
maintained these special ratios
among its fundamental processes.[100]

Pythagoras had hypothesized
that the right ratios between things generate music.
Physicists could now hypothesize
that the right ratios among cosmic powers
generate conscious self-awareness,
that the universe maintains
the ratios necessary to become aware of itself.[101]

None of this is proof.
It is all speculation.
But if this speculation turns out to be realistic,
it suggests that human mentality
is as fundamental to the universe
as the stars.
It suggests that in our work
of building a planetary mind,
we are participating with a universe
that was mindlike from the beginning.

In Dirac's vision of the universe as a whole,
we are not a fluke.
We are not an accident.
We are part of the self-awakening universe.
And our time for bringing forth
the planetary mind
is now at hand.

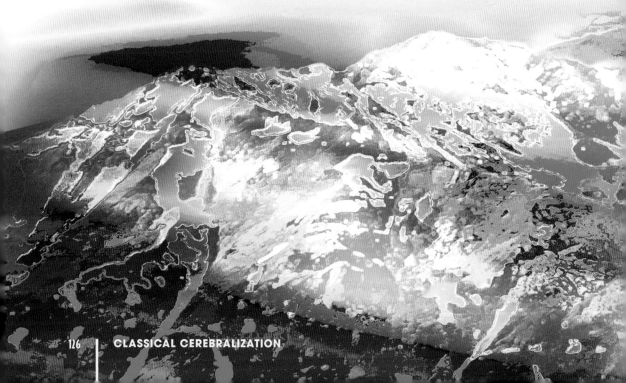

8

The Universe Aims at Harmonious Convergence

Throughout most of the Modern Era
scientists were unable to find convincing evidence
that there was a direction to cosmic evolution.
This ended in 1964
with the discovery of cosmic microwave background radiation.
Suddenly, we learned
that from the beginning of time,
the universe's development was inevitable.
Its rate of expansion
guaranteed the assembly of galaxies.
Its weak nuclear interaction made certain
the emergence of complex atoms.[102]
We now know the universe is going somewhere.
It advances toward its goal
through the actions of the entities
it constructs.
Now, after four hundred years of modern science,
it is possible to see
that the deepest aim,
residing in the heart of every entity,
is harmonious convergence.[103]

Consider Darwin's world-altering discovery
of biological evolution.
For three billion years,
life covered Earth's surface
in the form of single cells.
It is difficult for us today
to imagine this world,
because each of these single cells
is no bigger than the sharp point of a pin.
These tiny cells,
by exploring their relationships,
came together and constructed,
over evolutionary time,
bald eagles and forests of evergreen trees.

Something similar is happening with humanity.
For more than 99 percent of our existence,
we lived in hunter-gatherer bands,
each with a couple of dozen humans.
These humans interacted in various ways,
but they kept their simple structure intact,
generation after generation.
Then, the miracle of civilization happened.
Like cells converging and giving birth to complex forests,
the hunter-gatherer tribes converged
and spawned six great civilizations:
the Middle East,
China, India,
Northern Africa, Europe,
and Mesoamerica.

Convergence within the human journey
is neither easy nor automatic.
Consider East Asia several centuries before the Common Era.
Various states had been consumed in warfare
and had erected walls to protect themselves.
Finally, after more than two centuries of fighting,
the group led by Qin Shi Huang
subdued the rest.
His first act was to tear down the walls
separating the states.
He then used that same material
to make a single wall,
three thousand miles long,
protecting the extreme northern border
from attack by nomadic tribes.[104]

This historic move
led to a much larger gathering of humans.
Multiple ethnic groups
with diverse languages and cultures
were brought together.
They could begin to relate to each other
at a deeper level than warfare.
Qin Shi Huang had established the context
for the Chinese convergence
in which the arts, philosophy,
and literature all flourished,
where printing and paper were invented,
and where the great architecture
of the Summer Palace
and the Forbidden City
came forth.

We, today, are divided
into two hundred nation-states.
But the walls separating us
have been perforated
by international trade,
by internet communication,
by global media.
We are en route
to a harmonious convergence
of humanity as a whole.
The aim of harmonious convergence
was understood in its cosmic dimension
by Zhang Zai in the eleventh century:

Heaven is my father,
and Earth is my mother.
Even I, such a tiny thing,
find a place in their midst.
Therefore, that which fills Heaven and Earth,
I consider as my body;
that which directs Heaven and Earth,
I consider as my mind.
All people are my brothers and my sisters
all creatures are my companions.[105]

We do not know
how long it will take
for humanity to evolve
into a harmonious, flourishing, planetary community.
What we do know
is that this convergence
is the aim
of the noosphere
in our time.

MODERN

MODERN HEREDITY
Cosmic Evolution Manifesting as Humanity

<table>
<tr><td>1</td></tr>
</table>

The planetary mind is on the verge
of creating new human forms.
Hundreds of diverse hereditary traditions
are now entering
creative dialogue with one another.
As synergies are generated,
new and vibrant contexts
are put into place.
Over time, creative relationships
within these new contexts
will bring forth a million new human forms.

The first gathering of cultures
from all around the planet
took place in Chicago in 1893,
Representatives of Taoism, Buddhism, Islam,
and so forth,
traveled for weeks and even months
from their various continents
to be present.[106]

These cultural traditions
had developed in comparative isolation
for twenty-five hundred years.
Following this initial meeting in Chicago,
the dialogue developed so rapidly
that when a second meeting was called
a hundred years later in 1993,
representatives of all the world's religions
could be found living right there in Chicago.

We need to understand this planetary event
from the perspective of biology.
Homo sapiens are sometimes referred to
as a bio-cultural species
in that we are constrained
both by the DNA of biological heredity
and by the cultural coding
of our place of birth and development.[107]
For instance, our genetic inheritance from reptiles
awakens in us
the ability to see or run.
Our genetic inheritance from mammals
evokes in us
the emotional bonds represented by
the mother nursing her infant.[108]
Similarly, our minds
are activated in various ways
by the cultural codes of our place.
Two humans,
though virtually identical in a genetic sense,
will express their existence in distinct ways
if, for instance,
one of them is raised in Navajo culture,
and the other, in Muslim culture.

The infrastructure of the Modern period
has enabled cultures
from every place and time
to enter into dialogue.
Each of these cultures,
including the nine classical religions,
the five thousand Indigenous nations,
the philosophical and spiritual traditions
of the Modern world,
including feminism, environmentalism, existentialism,
gender studies, anarchism, and steady-state economism—
each of these cultures
contains unique and necessary wisdom.
As these rich and diverse traditions
interact with one another,
the potencies for human life
grow exponentially.
We are at a threshold
for a tremendous surge
in human creativity.

This explosion of bio-culturally distinct humans
will not be contained within any one civilization
or any particular thought tradition.
Henceforth, we will not be comfortable
defining ourselves as only Christian,
or only Zulu,
or only Chinese.
The dialogue of Earth's traditions
has the power to differentiate humanity
in radical ways.

We are deeply the same
at the genetic level,
with our need for water, food, and shelter,
but as we move further
into the twenty-first century,
each of us will discover,
in the synergy of cultures,
new possibilities
for how to become human.

Sacred scriptures from around the planet
help us discover who we are.
The lifeways of Indigenous nations
help us discover how to live.
So too, with the visionary works
of artists, musicians, and philosophers.
But our personalities will be unique.
The planetary mind rises
as each human person
gives birth to their one-and-only expression of life,
an expression that has never before existed,
a unique form of human life
that each of us brings forth.

MODERN TOOLS
2 The Magnificent Power of Paper

Many mythologies of the ancient world
imagined a universe created by a supreme being
all at once,
in the past.[109]
When the creation was finished,
creativity was finished too.

The key difference
between these ancient perspectives
and the view of contemporary science
is that we now know
creativity is incessant
and pervasive throughout time and space.[110]

Cosmic evolution is analogous
to the sequential development of organs
in a human embryo.[111]

The universe begins
with the construction of the simple atoms,
then moves to the building of galaxies,
then to the accretion of rocky planets,
and so forth, up to our present state.
Some structures of the world,
such as ants or the Olympic Mountains,
hold steady for millions of years.
But other structures,
especially humanity,
are in the midst of their development,
and thus, are a focal point
for the creativity of the universe.

Each moment of human existence
is a pulse of experience
containing sensory perceptions
of sight and sound,
as well as memories of former events.
There is the presence
of something else, as well—
novel potencies,
flashes of possibility.[112]

The challenge is effervescence.
We live in a sea of potency,
each moment presencing realities
that have never existed before.
And we sometimes experience
deep and significant insights
that disappear
as quickly as they emerge.
Truly new insights have no structure
to hold them steady in existence.
That is why even profound insights
can quickly slip away.

This condition of human existence
was irreversibly changed
by a novel technology
that could capture effervescent ideas:
the invention by Renaissance Italians
of readily accessible paper.[113]

With sheets of paper,
they kept track of their thinking,
and thus, novel potencies
found a foothold
in the flow of time.
Henceforth, humans could complexify their thinking
because they could build upon former thoughts.
This gave birth to an upwelling
of art, music,
new designs for government and architecture,
and new visions
of what it means to be human.

In the primordial fireball,
the novel potency was the galaxy.
In the early molten Earth,
the novel potency was life.
In the churning world of the twenty-first century,
the novel potency is the noosphere.

Humanity is creating the noosphere
from its imagination.
In this work,
we are no longer restricted
to our local communities.
We have, with the internet,
a new technology
that offers us the possibility
of forming relationships
throughout the planet.
Even the rarest of novelties
can now find resonance
with at least some small part
of the Earth community.
We have thus entered an era
of the most explosive creativity
in the history of the world.
The possibilities before us
are amazing.

MODERN REFLECTION
Time-Developmental Consciousness

The greatest discovery
in all of modern science
came in the twentieth century.
We live not in a fixed cosmos,
but in an ongoing cosmogenesis—
a universe in the process of complexification.
This discovery leads to the amazing realization
that we humans
and we universe
are constantly developing.
As we take in the reality of cosmogenesis,
we enter a new form of consciousness,
a time-developmental consciousness.
Some scholars regard this
as the most significant transformation of consciousness
in the last two million years
of hominid intelligence.[114]

The most convincing evidence
that we live in a cosmogenesis
was found in 1964
when Arno Penzias and Robert Wilson,
at Bell Labs in Holmdel, New Jersey,
detected light from 13.8 billion years ago.[115]
They were the first humans
to see back in time
to a much simpler universe,
a universe composed
of nothing more complex
than atoms of hydrogen and helium.

In order to appreciate what is meant
by "time-developmental consciousness,"
imagine Penzias and Wilson
in their laboratory
accompanied by a chimpanzee.
The chimpanzee's DNA
is 99 percent identical to theirs.
In addition, there are no new elements
in the human brain.
Thus, at the level of both genes and brains,
humans and chimpanzees
are profoundly alike.

But the experience of the chimpanzee,
as compared to the experience
of Penzias and Wilson,
is quite different.

A chimpanzee sitting next to Penzias and Wilson
would experience a hissing sound
produced by the technological instrumentation
that was transforming faint light rays
from the beginning of the universe
into sound.
Maybe the chimpanzee
would interpret this hissing
as coming from a snake
or some unseen waterfall.
But for Penzias and Wilson,
the experience was different.
They heard, in the hissing sound,
the earliest moments of the universe.
Even though their brains, eyes, and ears
were substantially the same
as those of the chimpanzee,
they had something not available
to the chimpanzee.
They had Einstein's General Theory of Relativity.
They had the theory of the origin of the universe,
as articulated by Georges Lemaître.
They were using these and other achievements
of human thought
to conceive something amazing:
humans, chimpanzees, and all other beings
are direct descendants
of the cosmic microwave radiation
they were listening to.

Take a moment and reflect
on this world-changing event.
These two humans
employed a radio telescope
to examine the early universe
at the very start
of its long and complicated process
of composing humans.
Penzias and Wilson had made contact
with the creative process
that would eventually bring them
into existence.
Their discovery shed light
on what it means to be human.
Humanity is that species
that enables the universe
to become aware of itself.[116]

The transition
from cosmos to cosmogenesis
is ongoing and disruptive.
Chaos accompanies
all transformations of consciousness.
It will be confusing.
It will be demanding.
But we must not allow
the depth of this challenge
to discourage us.
Every small step we take
participates in the unrelenting cosmic advance.

If our *Story of the Noosphere*
has ignited in you
just one brief moment of awareness,
the universe has awakened
because of your participation
in the profound process
of advancing the thinking layer of Earth,
the noosphere.

4

MODERN COMMUNICATION
Dialogue as the Pathway to Earth's Dream

Electronic communication systems
are on the verge of becoming
a central nervous system
for the Earth community.
The essential step
for this to take place
is a planet-wide dialogue
on what constitutes
true human happiness.
We participate
in the central creative energy
of our solar system
when we ask ourselves the crucial questions:
"What activities are right?
What activities are good?"

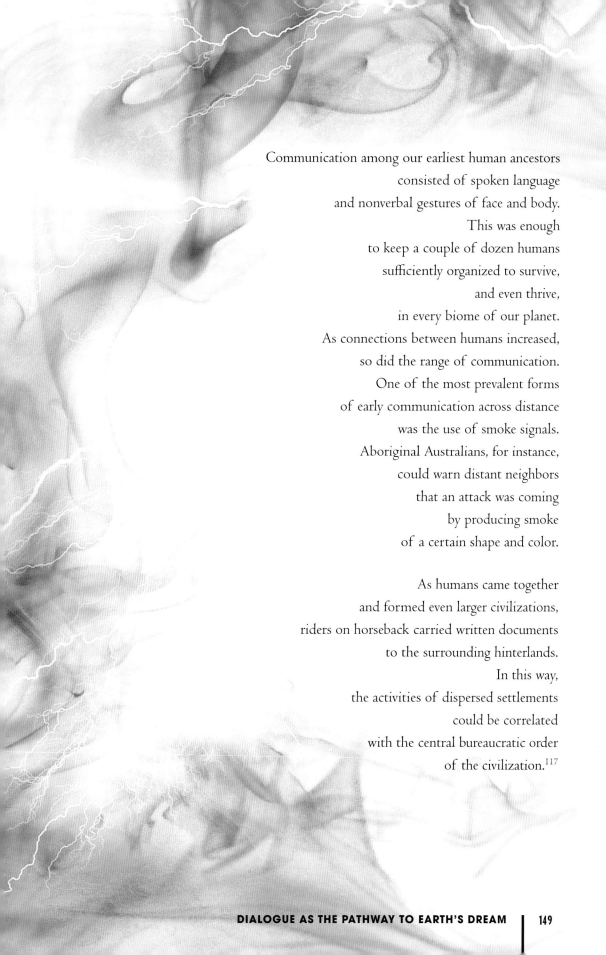

Communication among our earliest human ancestors
consisted of spoken language
and nonverbal gestures of face and body.
This was enough
to keep a couple of dozen humans
sufficiently organized to survive,
and even thrive,
in every biome of our planet.
As connections between humans increased,
so did the range of communication.
One of the most prevalent forms
of early communication across distance
was the use of smoke signals.
Aboriginal Australians, for instance,
could warn distant neighbors
that an attack was coming
by producing smoke
of a certain shape and color.

As humans came together
and formed even larger civilizations,
riders on horseback carried written documents
to the surrounding hinterlands.
In this way,
the activities of dispersed settlements
could be correlated
with the central bureaucratic order
of the civilization.[117]

The crucial step in the development
of global communication technology
was initiated by the July 1962 launch
of the Telstar satellite.
With Telstar, our messages could travel
beyond the curvature of the horizon.
For the first time in human history,
people in North America and Europe
entered into direct relationship
via television and telephone.
Internet connectivity and geostationary satellites
characterize our current moment,
a time when virtually every place on Earth
is in constant and instantaneous contact
with every other place on Earth.

The Earth community
has constructed a global organism
with a nervous system
similar to that of a sea jelly.
The parts of a sea jelly's body
are in electrical contact with other parts,
but no one part has central control.
That is to say, the sea jelly,
even though it has a nervous system,
does not have a brain.[118]

What about the Earth community?
Is our global communication system
going to stay at the level
of a sea jelly's nervous system?
Perhaps not.
Something more powerful could be at hand.
The human collective
could be developing as a nervous system with a brain.
To bring forth this global brain,
humanity needs to discover a common aim, a *telos*,
and to act in conscious alignment with it.[119]

Is there a common aim
for humanity's development?
Is there an aim, the pursuit of which,
leads to human happiness for all?
To answer this question,
we need only enter into creative dialogue,
a form of communication
that faces disagreements without evasion
and opens a dynamic
in which all points of view are explored.

Not only does dialogue facilitate
the bridging of fragmented disciplines,
it also crosses the chasm
separating so many human groups,
including the oppressed and marginalized.
Bringing fragments together
in dialogic relationship
is the work of love
and gives rise to the development
of humanity as a whole.

We have every reason to hope
for success in this endeavor.
Each individual and each group
will have democratized access
to all knowledge
in the emerging noosphere,
and thus, will be drawing from the intelligence
of the entire human collective.
Just as the relationships
between hydrogen atoms
led to the emergence of stars and galaxies,
and just as the relationships
between individual cells
led to the emergence of blue whales and hummingbirds,
so too, in creative dialogue,
the deepening relationships among human groups
will lead to our common aim, our *telos*.
As humanity embraces this common aim,
the Earth community enters fully
into the era of conscious evolution.

5 | A One-Hundred-Thousand-Year Experiment

An amazing experiment
requiring a hundred thousand years
suggests that the major stages
of humanity's development
were set from the very beginning.
The experiment was initiated
when *Homo sapiens* began to flow north
out of Africa.
Some veered to the west
and populated Europe.
Others turned right
and crossed over into the Americas.
The key point to ponder
is that although the humans settling in Europe
had utterly no contact
with the humans trekking toward the Americas,
when they met in the sixteenth century,
one hundred thousand years later,
they found they had evolved
through profoundly similar stages.

Archaeologists have recently concluded
that in the thirteenth century,
the population of Cahokia,
a Native American city near present-day St. Louis, Missouri,
matched that of contemporaneous London
and far exceeded that of Paris.[120]
This comes as a shock
to those of us educated in the West
whose focus has been on the humans
who settled in Europe and the Middle East.
We've substantially ignored
the earliest Americans because,
so we believed,
they hadn't advance into civilization
as the European humans had.
For example, we were certain the early Americans
did not leave written records.
But even this assumption was proven false
when scholars, in the latter part of the twentieth century,
came to realize that the Mayans
had invented a written language
entirely on their own,
that is, entirely independent
of the inventions of writing
that took place in Mesopotamia,
China, and North Africa.[121]

This one-hundred-thousand-year experiment
of disparate human groups
developing independently
enables us to speak with authority
about the so-called natural development of humanity.
Complexity scientists now regard
development as inevitable
when the geometry of a dynamical system
has what is called a "basin of attraction."[122]
That is, even though dynamical systems
include chance events,
there can also be a structural geometry in phase space
that draws the system forward to a final form.

For instance, complexity science understands
the form of the fruiting oak tree
as drawing the acorn into the taproot,
and then, into the sapling,
and then, into the mature, adult form.
Some complexity scientists
now regard the noosphere
as the form that is drawing human populations
through their sequential development.
Humans began inside conscious self-awareness,
then were drawn to construct spoken languages,
then learned to cultivate seeds,
then found the skill to conjure up written language.
Throughout this development,
it is the noosphere
as the basin of attraction
that draws the dynamical system forward,
even into the major disruptions
we are experiencing today.

The phrase "major disruptions"
is not meant in a moral sense,
but refers to the chaos
that takes place in nonlinear systems
as they move through phase changes.
The emergence of modern humans
equipped with powerful technologies
has brought Earth into its present zone of chaos.
In dynamical terms,
we are living in a time
when even minor events
can have immense long-term effects.

An analogy for our situation
that comes from chemistry
is the supersaturated solution.
Just before crystallization,
the chemist has only to toss
a tiny seed into the solution
and the crystal irrupts into existence.[123]

For those of us
who wish to participate consciously
in this historic transition,
the first requirement
is to see through the noise.
The divisions, fighting, and polarizations
of our time
are the symptoms of our having entered
a critical phase transition.
Chaos is inevitable.
Core assumptions of modern civilization
are disintegrating.
We no longer regard the universe
as a mechanical process
governed by outside laws.
Nor are we inspired
by the belief that the universe is meaningless
or the notion that human existence is an absurdity.

The well-being
of every sentient species of life
now depends upon us.
We are not separate from one another.
We are, in fact, composed of each other,
and in this profound communion,
we are destined to make a leap in being
that brings forth a new era
of flourishing Earth community.

6 The Noospheric Nourishment of Modern Trade

With the challenges besetting our Earth community,
A vision of an emerging planetary mind can seem naive.
It is understandable that pessimism
has captured so many of us.
To avoid sinking into depression and despair,
we need to take in the larger arc of history.
In the Modern Era,
trading networks exploded
and improved the fabric of human life.
A keen appreciation
of what trade has bequeathed to us
strengthens our understanding
of the noosphere's emergence.

We need to ask the question:
Has human life improved over the last two thousand years?
The answer is both yes and no.
No, because modern industrial society
has regarded Earth
as an assemblage of natural resources
for human use.[124]
A dualistic consciousness
has resulted in ecological destruction
throughout the planet,
the reality of which
we are now painfully aware.
But the answer is also a resounding *yes*.
Life for *Homo sapiens*
has improved dramatically,
and this, too, needs to be noted.

The historian Angus Maddison
at the University of Groningen
has calculated the world's per capita income
from the beginning of the Common Era
up to our day.[125]
For the first eighteen hundred years,
there was only a modest increase.
The lifestyle for serfs
remained approximately the same
throughout these centuries.
Which is to say,
life for the vast majority of humans
consisted of the backbreaking work
of medieval agriculture.

Then, something amazing happened.
From the nineteenth to the twenty-first centuries,
there was a tenfold increase
in per capita production of goods.
On average, a person today
has access to ten times
the amount of education,
cultural activities, medical care, clothing,
food, transportation, and housing
that was available to people
just two centuries ago.

This explosion of goods and services
as a result of increased productivity
came in large part when we discovered
powerful ways for moving materials and products
through our trade networks.
For instance, with the invention
of the high-pressure steam engine,
European engineers sent trains across the continents.
The discovery of steel alloy
led to the building of oceangoing ships
that could carry a thousand times more cargo
than the largest wooden ships of the Middle Ages.

With this increase in the movement of goods,
the noosphere was establishing
a circulatory system of nourishment
which led to richer lifestyles
and relationships not previously possible.

Consider the opportunities for connection
between people in different civilizations
during the early Middle Ages.
Leaders in China established agreements
with merchants in the Roman Empire
so that goods could flow back and forth
on the Silk Road.

But a caravan of camels
required two years for a round trip,
and communication between encounters
was necessarily sparse.
In contrast, consider our situation today:
Agreements between distant humans
are worked out in real time via video conferencing.
Traders in Vietnam have relationships
with traders in Seattle,
as if they lived in the same neighborhood.

Had we been born in the year 1200 CE,
we would, in all likelihood,
be living the difficult and barren life of serfdom.
That we, today, are not serfs
is the work of humans
who had a deep faith
in humanity's ability to create
thriving communities of life.
We now know that this faith
is faith in human creativity.
And faith in human creativity
is faith in the noosphere.

In our universe
there is always something more to learn.[126]
And with new knowledge,
we are empowered to repair our ecosystems
and enrich the lives of all beings.
This is the attitude of those individuals
who have done the most to improve our lives.
The major advances of humanity
have come from the optimists.

7 The Stupendous Power of the James Webb Space Telescope

The construction and launch
of the James Webb Space Telescope
is one of the most spectacular illustrations of cerebralization,
the noosphere's ability to build a planetary mind.

A critical discovery
for the work of building the space telescope
took place in 1687,
when Isaac Newton published
the universal law of gravitation.
His equations worked with great accuracy
and were filled with surprises,
including the amazing discovery
by Joseph-Louis Lagrange in 1772
while analyzing the so-called three-body problem.
Lagrange found five equilibrium points
in the Earth-sun system
where the forces balance out.[127]
He proved, in theory, that if a body was placed
precisely at one of these five points,
it would remain stationary
relative to the sun and Earth.

Two centuries later,
we have made the journey
to one of these places.
On December 25, 2021,
the James Webb Space Telescope was launched
in the direction of the Lagrange point
ninety-four million miles from the sun.
This endeavor is leading
to the most comprehensive gathering of cosmic data
in the history of the world.
The sensitivity of the telescope's instruments
allows for the detection of light emitted
at the formation
of the earliest galaxies.

To see the relevance
of the space telescope to cerebralization,
we need to imagine its construction
in terms of the most basic dynamic in the universe,
the dual action of dispersal and contraction.[128]
The universe began
with the dispersal of the primordial plasma.
This was followed by subsets of plasma
contracting into stars and galaxies.

Then, within each galaxy,
stars exploded and dispersed elements
into clouds that later collapsed
into solar systems with planets.
Next, living cells emerged
and spread over the Earth's surface.
Then, three billion years later,
subsets of these cells gathered together
into complex multicellular organisms.
At each stage of development,
the same dispersal and contraction dynamism
was at work.

Humans evolved inside this dynamism.
We began by dispersing over the surface of Earth,
and then, came together
around common meanings and goals.
The James Webb Space Telescope
is an example.
Over the last three decades,
engineers from fourteen countries
brought their minds together,
along with atoms of beryllium, aluminum, and gold,
and constructed a telescope,
a hundred times more sentient than the Hubble.[129]

This entire sequence can be seen
as a process of cerebralization.
The sun, Earth, and the Webb Telescope
form a kind of body, a hyperbody.[130]

The telescope is the eye.
Humanity is the mind
that controls the eye.
Just as our individual brains
send electronic messages
to muscles that focus our eyeballs,
so, too, do technicians at NASA
send electronic messages
to Webb's gyroscopes
that position its instruments.
The sun, Earth, and telescope
form a stable, mindlike process
that enables the universe
to become more aware of itself.

To see the significance of this,
reflect back to the Paleolithic.
The humans alive then
had the same brain we have.
They had the same desire
to learn the nature of reality.
Now, think of the monumental acceleration
the learning process
has undergone through time.
No Paleolithic human
could imagine the James Webb Space Telescope.
It was imagined and built
by the noosphere.

If we personify the noosphere
in order to make a point,
we can say the noosphere built
the James Webb Space Telescope
in order to satisfy
its desire to know.
This desire to know
is one of the primordial desires.
There are others as well.
We desire to heal,
to educate, to love, to feed the hungry,
and to bring laughter and joy
to those who suffer.
Just as the noosphere
builds telescopes in order to know,
it works to satisfy
all of the primordial desires.

We don't know the details
of how the noosphere
will ultimately satisfy
each of the primordial desires.
We are like Paleolithic humans
trying to imagine the James Webb Space Telescope.
Even so, we can catch glimmers of the future.
We can begin to suss out the pathways.
Dedication to creative work
is grounded in faith
that we are building solutions
just as elegant, in their own way,
as the space telescope.
We are ensconced in a noosphere
that is bringing forth
a world that will amaze.

8 | Convergence to a Unified Humanity

The convergence taking place
in humanity today
is just as significant
as the emergence of life
four billion years ago.

When we reflect
on the whole sweep
of cosmic evolution,
we see how convergence
is a fundamental dynamic
of the universe.[131]
In fact, the deepest meaning of existence
can be captured
with a three-word sentence:
Convergence ignites novelty.[132]

Convergence began
when clouds of hydrogen and helium
collapsed into stars.
This collapse ignited stellar nucleosynthesis
where the primal atoms of hydrogen and helium
fused into more complex forms
of oxygen, carbon, and phosphorus.

When these elements were released
into the galaxy,
a second stage of convergence began.
Clouds enriched with these chemical elements
collapsed into stellar systems
that created the first rocky planets.

It was on these rocky planets
that a third stage took place,
one that reveals the sheer magic of convergence.
Reflect on the journey of oxygen.
Before the appearance of rocky planets,
oxygen had been floating about
in the clouds of every galaxy.
Only on the tiny rocky planets
would oxygen combine with other elements
and become oceans,
granite mountains,
and galloping horses.

Humans are learning to recognize
the amazing capacity of matter
to bring forth novelty.
We are stunned by the cosmic creativity
drawing living beings out of molten rock.
Who could have guessed
that rocks had the power
to come alive?

Many philosophers have a technical word
for the realm of possibilities.
Aristotle used the Greek word *dunamis*.
In the twenty-first century,
quantum philosopher Timothy Eastman
uses the Latin word *potentiae*.[133]
In *Story of the Noosphere*,
we use the phrase "extraordinary realm."
Though different words are used,
many philosophers and scientists agree
that reality is more than the *actual entities*[134]
existing in any one moment.
Reality consists of actual entities
together with the infinite possibilities
held in the extraordinary realm.
Only by considering the extraordinary realm
are we in touch
with the full reality
of our world.

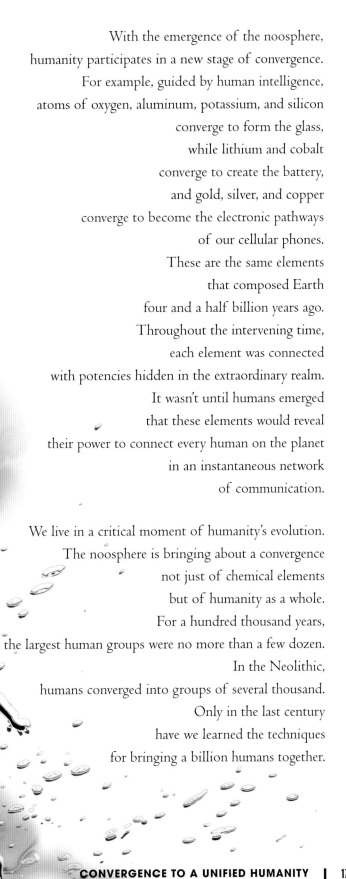

With the emergence of the noosphere,
humanity participates in a new stage of convergence.
For example, guided by human intelligence,
atoms of oxygen, aluminum, potassium, and silicon
converge to form the glass,
while lithium and cobalt
converge to create the battery,
and gold, silver, and copper
converge to become the electronic pathways
of our cellular phones.
These are the same elements
that composed Earth
four and a half billion years ago.
Throughout the intervening time,
each element was connected
with potencies hidden in the extraordinary realm.
It wasn't until humans emerged
that these elements would reveal
their power to connect every human on the planet
in an instantaneous network
of communication.

We live in a critical moment of humanity's evolution.
The noosphere is bringing about a convergence
not just of chemical elements
but of humanity as a whole.
For a hundred thousand years,
the largest human groups were no more than a few dozen.
In the Neolithic,
humans converged into groups of several thousand.
Only in the last century
have we learned the techniques
for bringing a billion humans together.

The convergence happening now
is the ongoing unification
of humanity at a planetary level.

Potencies that have swirled about each human
are being actualized by this convergence,
giving rise to qualities just as surprising
as the emergence of life
out of rocks.
Qualities such as mutual understanding,
comprehensive compassion,
forgiveness—
these potencies have been hovering
in the extraordinary realm
since the beginning.
Now is the time they arise
and ripple throughout the planet.
This convergence of peoples
into a unified humanity
will change everything.

POSTSCRIPT

Through several dozen chapters, we have detailed the rise and deepening of the noosphere from the Paleolithic to the present. What a vast journey humanity has been on.

We can summarize our book with a single phrase: *Our chapters are an exploration of the evolutionary potentiality of humanity.*

A dramatic way to point to our cosmic potential is to compare our journey to our ape relatives. At a genetic level, *Homo sapiens* and chimpanzees are 99 percent identical. Now, consider that over the last hundred thousand years, humans spread throughout the planet, learned the processes of their biology, articulated the mathematical laws of the cosmos, explored the oceans, identified continental drift, changed the atmosphere, constructed ten thousand cities, flew to the moon, assembled libraries, transformed the biosphere, and launched communication satellites so that each human being can be instantaneously connected to the rest of humanity.

During that same interval of time, the chimpanzees did not change. They did not move from equatorial Africa. They remained identical to their ancestors. The chasm between these two species—chimpanzees and humans—provides insight into the meaning and purpose of humanity.

Humans are carrying out a planetary transformation from a living planet to a thinking Earth. With differing degrees of awareness, each of us engages in this work. The recent construction and launch of the James Webb Space Telescope provides an illustration of the collective nature of creativity. No individual human could construct the Webb telescope—not Einstein, not Plato, not Genghis Khan. No individual human has the mental capacity or knowledge to perform such a task; only a unified humanity does. Engineers from fourteen different countries worked together to build it. All of them were essential to the task. So, too, were the teachers who introduced these engineers to vast systems of knowledge accumulated by humans over many centuries. None of the individual engineers could have come up with such detailed knowledge on their own. The political leaders were also essential, for they maintained the order in our societies necessary for human development. Billions of humans in unison can look upon the magnificent James Webb Space Telescope and say together, "We built it."

What is true of the James Webb Space Telescope is true for the noosphere as a whole. All humans, whether they are fully aware of it, are architects of this new superorganism. To appreciate this, we must understand that our lives have dual dimensions. We might be a person working for the phone company, a mediator at a crisis center, a programmer at a Silicon Valley startup, or a train dispatcher for Canadian National; if so, we are, at the very same time, a noospheric advance in the aspects of communication, convergence, tools, and trade.

There will be flashes when the noospheric dimensions of your life become clear, and you will realize, with amazement, that you are the actual, creative energy of the universe. This astonishment will subside as you return to the individualistic consciousness of late modernity. The aim is not to escape individualistic consciousness with all its powers. The aim is to develop the capacity to move spontaneously between individualistic and noospheric consciousness. That is how the great work of the noosphere continues.

We must bear in mind that the way forward will include great hardship. What we are asked to do is difficult, almost beyond imagination. But such has always been the case. Every major transformation of the universe has seemed entirely unrealistic at the outset. Consider the challenge of bringing forth life from rocks. Imagine initiating a process that would eventually change bacteria into elephants. Our challenge is equally daunting. The recalcitrant materials we have to work with are not rocks or bacteria but a deficient, war-torn consciousness. Our challenge is to stay faithful to the long process that will, over time, unify the antagonistic fragments of humanity.

Separated from each other, we fall into lower levels of awareness, including cynicism and depression. From such meager states of mind, we convince ourselves that nothing can be done to change the situation—that all efforts to improve the world are wasted energy. Such pessimism fails to consider that change is constant throughout the fourteen billion years of cosmogenesis. The way out of despair is through relationships with those who see what is taking place. Connected with one another, we find both the heroic commitment and the profound creativity necessary to bring forth a unified humanity.

NOTES

1. A gradual transition and a complex network of species characterize human evolution. *Australopithecus afarensis*, including the famous specimen "Lucy," is among the earliest well-documented hominins for which we have reliable brain and body size estimates. There has yet to be direct evidence in the fossil record that *Australopithecus afarensis* was specifically preyed upon by large cats or any other predator. However, some inferences can be made based on ecological context and comparisons with modern ecosystems. Modern primates are occasionally preyed upon by large cats. Since *Australopithecus afarensis* shares some ecological similarities with modern primates, it is plausible to consider that predation or potential encounters with large carnivores could have occurred. Donald C. Johanson, Tim D. White, and Yves Coppens, "A New Species of the Genus *Australopithecus* (Primates: Hominidae) from the Pliocene of Eastern Africa," *Kirtlandia*, no. 28 (1978): 2–14, https://biostor.org/reference/193077.

2. Yuval Harari, professor at the Hebrew University in Jerusalem and author of *Sapiens: A Brief History of Humankind*, attributes the successful spread of *Homo sapiens* "all over the world" to their unique ability to "cooperate both flexibly and in very large numbers." What allows us to do that, he believes, is our imagination and our ability not only to imagine things but to share and spread fictional stories. "This is why we can cooperate in our billions whereas chimpanzees cannot, and why we have reached the moon and split the atom and deciphered DNA, and they just play with sticks and bananas." "Why Did Humans Become the Most Successful Species on Earth?" NPR's *TED Radio Hour*, hosted by Guy Raz, https://www.npr.org/transcripts/468882620.

3. Research suggests that ending the day around the campfire, where songs, stories, and relationships flourished, ultimately shaped human cultures and may have contributed significantly to the development of our capacity for understanding one another, cooperating, and internalizing culture. Anthropologist Polly Wiessner reached these conclusions after spending 174 days living with the Ju/'hoan (! Kung) Bushmen of Botswana and Namibia. Wiessner contrasted recorded content of daytime conversations with that of nighttime discussions and found that, while work-related chatter and gossip accounted for three-quarters of daytime conversation, nighttime dialogue was more than 80 percent centered on singing, dancing, spirituality, and "enthralling stories, often about known people," including tales about "the exploits of distant kin, adventures in towns, local politics, truck stories, elephant stories, or experiences in trance." Nighttime gatherings around the campfire provided a relatively leisurely period where individuals could engage in prolonged conversations. The absence of immediate tasks or distractions could have allowed

for more in-depth discussions and the exploration of abstract or imaginative ideas, with body language dimmed and facial expressions accentuated by flickering flames. As such, the campfire likely contributed significantly to developing and transmitting linguistic creativity, including the formation of new words, expressions, and narrative structures. See Polly W. Wiessner, edited by Robert Whallon, "Embers of Society: Firelight Talk among the Ju/' hoansi Bushmen," *Proceedings of the National Academy of Sciences* III, no. 39 (September 2014): 14027–35, https://doi.org/10.1073/pnas.1404212111.

4. German philosopher Wolfgang Leidhold emphasizes the importance of symbols in what he calls "the turn to imagination." Symbols enable us to access and engage with the imaginative realm, where we can transcend the boundaries of time, space, and immediate reality. Through symbolic language, we can evoke vivid mental images, create narratives, and explore alternative possibilities. Wolfgang Leidhold, *The History of Experience: A Study in Experiential Turns and Cultural Dynamics from the Paleolithic to the Present Day* (New York: Routledge, 2023), 30.

5. Anthropologists from University College London report that the Agta people, a community of hunter-gatherers in the Philippines, use stories to impart values, lessen conflict, and foster cooperation. They found cooperative behavior was highest in the camps with the most skilled storytellers. They also learned that the tribe's most skilled storytellers were more well-liked and had higher reproductive success than the best hunters and foragers. In other words, natural selection dynamics seem to favor the ability to tell a good story. Daniel Smith et al., "Cooperation and the Evolution of Hunter-Gatherer Storytelling," *Nature Communications* 8, no. 1 (December 2017): 1–9, https://doi.org/10.1038/s41467-017-02036-8.

6. The Human Energy project delineates three stories of the universe, each with its own assumptions and distinct worldview. The first story designates worldviews centered on mythic narrative and ritual enactment, including the thought that prevails in contemporary religions and idealisms. The second story emphasizes mathematical models, universal laws, the natural sciences, modern technology, and materialist reductionism. Prigogine and Stengers point out that Western thought oscillates between these two stories: one, an idealist reductionism in which God governs the universe, and the other, a materialist reductionism that understands the "world as an automaton." They observe, "In fact, these visions are connected. An automaton needs an external god." See Ilya Prigogine and Isabelle Stengers, *Order Out of Chaos: Man's New Dialogue with Nature* (New York: Bantam Books, 1984), 6–7. Human Energy's "Third Story" is a new attempt to "envision a worldview that integrates the meaning, purpose, and ethical dimension of First Story logic with the universality, clarity of method, and applicability inherent in Second Story logic." See Human Energy, "The Three Stories of the Universe," https://humanenergy.io/the-three-stories-of-the-universe.

7. While the specific "one thousand" factor might be a point of contention and debate among scientists, there is no doubt that the interplay between our biology and our ability to disseminate and build upon knowledge rapidly has accelerated the pace of change. One has only to compare humanity's achievement of the capacity for sustained flight to the evolutionary development of flying in the bat, the only group of mammals capable of sustained flight. The evolution of flight-capable bats from small tree-dwelling, gliding mammals is estimated to have spanned several million years. In contrast, little more

than one thousand years span the development of human flight from the early gliders of the ninth and eleventh centuries to Orville Wright's first controlled, sustained flight in a powered airplane on December 17, 1903. See Jane Harbidge, "Flying through the Ages," BBC News, March 19, 1999, http://news.bbc.co.uk/2/hi/special_report/1998/11/98/great_balloon_challenge/299568.stm. Moreover, cultural evolution has enhanced, not eliminated, biological evolution. Genetic adaptation is increasing rapidly in response to the challenges of increased population and changing culture. John Hawks et al., "Recent Acceleration of Human Adaptive Evolution," *Proceedings of the National Academy of Sciences of the United States of America* 104, no. 52 (December 2007): 20753–58, https://doi.org/10.1073/pnas.0707650104.

8. Fire is a combustion process requiring oxygen and fuel, which are present in sufficient concentrations on Earth but not elsewhere in our solar system.

9. Research suggests that cooking food led to a rapid increase in brain size in human evolution. The reasoning is as follows: Larger mammals generally have larger brains. Nevertheless, the great ape, the largest of primates, does not have the largest primate brain, and the smaller-statured *Homo erectus*, leading to *Homo sapiens*, has among the largest hominid brains, certainly larger than the primates. Increased brain size comes with an energetic cost that requires more hours spent feeding. Great apes eat primarily low-calorie raw foods, presenting a metabolic limitation to possible brain size relative to body size: the number of hours available for feeding. *Homo erectus* overcame this metabolic limitation to its number of brain neurons when it shifted to cooked food, thus yielding far more calories per hour spent feeding. Karina Fonseca-Azevedo and Suzana Herculano-Houzel, "Metabolic Constraint Imposes Tradeoff between Body Size and Number of Brain Neurons in Human Evolution," *Proceedings of the National Academy of Sciences* 109, no. 45 (October 2012): 18571–76, https://doi.org/10.1073/pnas.1206390109.

10. Neoteny refers to slowed or delayed development and the retention of ancestral juvenile features by the adults in a lineage. The classic example of neoteny is the axolotl, a salamander that retains its juvenile gills all its life and does not undergo the metamorphosis characteristic of other salamanders. The domestic dog is also neotenous, behaving more like a wolf pup than an adult wolf for most of its life. Thinkers as diverse as the prominent evolutionary biologist Stephen Jay Gould and the anthropologist and humanist Ashley Montagu understand neoteny as an overarching explanation of human evolution. See Stephen Jay Gould, *Ontogeny and Phylogeny* (Cambridge, MA: Belknap Press of Harvard University Press, 1977); see also Ashley Montagu, *Growing Young*, 2nd ed. (Westport, CT: Bergin & Garvey, 1989). Indeed, the present authors speculate that neoteny may be an evolutionary activity of the universe occurring at all levels, a return-to-earlier-conditions that can enable the exploration of developmental potencies that once existed but, for whatever reason, were transient. For instance, in the core of a star, nuclear fusion processes occur that mirror, in a way, the conditions of the universe's infancy. Revisiting earlier states or conditions so that previous potentials might be explored anew is a recurring theme of the universe's story.

11. Epigenetics is the emerging area of scientific research that explores the heritable changes in gene expression that are not attributable to mutations in the sequence of DNA. By

way of the "epigenome," environmental influences affect whether and how genes are expressed, resulting in a kind of "Lamarckian inheritance." Epigenetic characteristics can be passed on epigenetically and become subject to the exact mechanisms of evolution as those with a purely genetic origin. See ETH Zurich, "Epigenetics: DNA Isn't Everything," *ScienceDaily*, April 13, 2009, https://www.sciencedaily.com/releases/2009/04/090412081315.htm.

12. Shizuyo Sutou, an expert in mutation research and professor of the Functional Genomics Laboratory at Shujitsu University, makes the argument that a semidominant single mutation known to induce the loss of body hair could be the driving force that separated humans from other primates five to seven million years ago. See Shizuyo Sutou, "Hairless Mutation: A Driving Force of Humanization from a Human–Ape Common Ancestor by Enforcing Upright Walking While Holding a Baby with Both Hands," *Genes to Cells* 17, no. 4 (2012): 264–72, https://doi.org/10.1111/j.1365-2443.2012.01592.x. So-called regulatory genes that control the expression of other genes may also play a crucial role in determining the overall structure of organisms and the timing of their development. While Hox genes primarily determine the spatial organization of body structures, determining where and how structures like limbs, vertebrae, and other body parts develop, other genes that interact with the HOX genes provide temporal information to embryonic cells that impacts when certain structures mature or reach their final form. Forkhead-box protein P2 (FOXP2), in particular, has been implicated in human evolution, especially as regards the development of language and speech and the plasticity of neuronal connections. While no single "neoteny gene" has been identified, two specific amino acid mutations in the FOXP2 protein distinguish modern humans from our closest primate ancestors. While the direct connection to neoteny remains speculative, research into how FOXP2 influences plasticity is ongoing. See Sonja C. Vernes et al., "Foxp2 Regulates Gene Networks Implicated in Neurite Outgrowth in the Developing Brain," *PLOS Genetics* 7, no. 7 (July 2011): e1002145, https://doi.org/10.1371/journal.pgen.1002145. See also Elizabeth Spiteri et al., "Identification of the Transcriptional Targets of FOXP2, a Gene Linked to Speech and Language, in Developing Human Brain," *American Journal of Human Genetics* 81, no. 6 (December 2007): 1144–57, https://doi:10.1086/522237.

13. Sociologist of religion Robert Bellah views play as central to the development of religious consciousness. Play is fundamental precisely because it provides an "extinction of time in time" or what Gordon Burghardt calls a "relaxed field" of alternative reality. Immersed in an alternative reality, new relations become possible, new dimensions of the universe are awakened, and creativity and conscious development become possible. Robert N. Bellah, *Religion in Human Evolution: From the Paleolithic to the Axial Age* (Cambridge, MA: The Belknap Press of Harvard University Press, 2011), 568–569, 76–77.

14. Neotenic characteristics found in humans as compared to primates are both physiological, i.e., relatively large heads, flat faces, lack of body hair, and late physical maturation; and behavioral, i.e., playfulness, curiosity, prolonged dependency, learning plasticity, emotional expressivity, and the deep and extended need for social bonding.

15. Imagining the universe's evolution taking place over a single year and symbolic communication appearing in the very last fraction of a second is a way to highlight the relatively recent emergence of symbolic communication in the broader timeline of cosmic

evolution. John F. Haught has another beautiful way to get a sense of the temporal immensity of the great epic of the universe. He asks us,

> Imagine that you have in your library a shelf containing thirty large books. Each volume is 450 pages long, and each page stands for one million years. The Big Bang takes place on page 1 of volume 1, and the first twenty-one books have to do only with lifeless physical, chemical, stellar, and galactic processes. Life is not in a hurry to make its entry into the story. Our solar system appears at the beginning of volume 21, about 4.5 billion years ago, but the early instances of life do not show up until volume 22 (3.8 billion years ago by many recent estimates). Life remains single-celled until toward the end of volume 29, where the Cambrian explosion occurs. At this point in the story, organisms begin to become increasingly complex at a more accelerated pace than ever before. Even so, dinosaurs do not show up until around the middle of volume 30, and they go extinct on page 384. Only the last 66 pages or so of volume 30 feature the flourishing of mammalian life. Human-like ancestors begin to show up a few pages from the end of volume 30, but anatomically modern humans make their appearance only about halfway down page 450. Self-reflective subjectivity, ethical aspiration, and the religious quest for rightness arrive in the universe only in the last paragraph of the last page of the last volume.

John F. Haught, *The New Cosmic Story: Inside Our Awakening Universe* (New Haven, CT: Yale University Press, 2017), 31.

16. The term "graviton" was coined by Soviet physicists Dmitri Blokhintsev and F. M. Gal'perin in 1934 to name a hypothetical mediator of gravitational interaction between elementary particles. The graviton is thought to mediate gravitational force in the framework of quantum field theory just as the three other known forces of nature are mediated by elementary particles: the electromagnetic force by photons, the strong interaction by gluons, and the weak interaction by bosons. The existence of the graviton is an assumption of contemporary Quantum Gravitation theory and the "Theory of Everything," yet while photons, gluons, and W and Z bosons have all been detected in experiments, the graviton remains elusive. The search for the graviton is an active area of research in theoretical physics and quantum gravity. See Dmitri I. Blokhintsev and F. M. Gal'perin, "Гипотеза нейтрино и закон сохранения" [Neutrino hypothesis and conservation of energy]," *Pod Znamenem Marxisma* (in Russian) 6 (1934): 147–57, cited in Firmin J. Oliveira, "The Principle of Equivalence: Periastron Precession, Light Deflection, Binary Star Decay, Graviton Temperature, Dark Matter, and Galaxy Rotation Curves," *Journal of High Energy Physics, Gravitation, and Cosmology* 7, no. 2 (April 2021): 661–79.

17. The study of plant communication and signaling is a rapidly growing area of research that continues to expand our understanding of plant capabilities and challenge our preconceptions about the plant kingdom. Research by molecular biologist František Baluška and renowned plant neurobiologist Stefano Mancuso demonstrates that plants possess remarkable capacities, including the ability to keep time, count, distinguish kin from strangers and competitors, discern the best patches of soil and sun, and chemically ward off enemies. See František Baluška and Stefano Mancuso, "Plant Neurobiology as a Paradigm Shift Not Only in the Plant Sciences," *Plant Signaling & Behavior* 2, no. 4 (2007):

205–7, doi:10.4161/psb.2.4.4550. Baluška and Susan J. Murch of the University of British Columbia argue that plants have a form of consciousness. If plants produce ethylene, a compound that renders humans and animals unconscious and living plants temporarily unresponsive to their environment, Baluška argues, then the *normal* state of a plant *must* be a form of consciousness. See František Baluška et al., "Understanding of Anesthesia—Why Consciousness Is Essential for Life and Not Based on Genes," *Communicative & Integrative Biology* 9, no. 6 (November 2016): e1238118, doi:10.1080/19420889.2016.1238118. Similarly, Murch asks the intriguing question, "Why would plants produce mood-altering and sleep-inducing compounds such as serotonin and melatonin?" See Susan J. Murch, C. B. Simmons, and P. K. Saxena, "Melatonin in Feverfew and Other Medicinal Plants," *Lancet* 350, no. 9091 (November 1997): 1598–99, DOI: 10.1016/S0140-6736(05)64014-7. Although the concept of mood as experienced by humans is difficult to attribute to plants, it is clear from decades of research by Murch and others that plants, like animals, produce compounds in response to their environment. See Susan J. Murch and Lauren A. E. Erland, "A Systematic Review of Melatonin in Plants: An Example of Evolution of Literature," *Frontiers in Plant Science* 12 (June 2021): 683047, https://www.frontiersin.org/journals/plant-science/articles/10.3389/fpls.2021.683047/full.

18. Terrence W. Deacon, anthropologist and cognitive scientist based at the University of California, Berkeley, in his book *The Symbolic Species: The Co-Evolution of Language and the Brain*, uses the alarm calls of velvet monkeys as an example of the phenomenon of referential signaling. Velvet monkeys emit different calls in response to various predators such as eagles, leopards, or snakes. The monkey's call is not merely an external correlate of an internal state, as might be argued by some animal behaviorists, but a distinct vocalization that refers to particular predators in the monkey's environment and calls for distinct escape behaviors. Deacon argues that referential signaling in human language evolved from these more basic forms of communication found in other animal species. Terrence W. Deacon, *The Symbolic Species: The Co-evolution of Language and the Brain* (New York: W. W. Norton & Company, 1997), 53–57.

19. Drawing upon the thought of Charles Sanders Peirce, Deacon argues that "all forms of thought (ideas) are essentially communication (transmission of signs), organized by an underlying logic (or semiotic …) that is not fundamentally different for communication processes inside or outside of brains." Three hierarchical categories of referential associations, or levels of reference, are used in the interpretive process to relate signs to what they signify: *iconic*, *indexical*, and *symbolic*. Deacon explains, "Symbolic relationships are composed of indexical relationships between sets of indices and indexical relationships are composed of iconic relationships between sets of icons." Thus, the indexical reference is a higher, more complex level of referential association than the iconic, and symbolic reference is higher still. Symbolic communication, derived from processes at work in the universe, is a fundamental aspect of human cognition and the driving force behind human cultural development, scientific advancement, and the formation of complex societies. Deacon, *The Symbolic Species*, 70, 75.

20. Several expansions of populations of the genus *Homo* out of Africa and throughout Eurasia took place in the Paleolithic between 2.1 million and 200,000 years ago, in contrast to the later expansion of *Homo sapiens,* which likely began 200,000 or so years ago. These earlier dispersals of ancient hominins have been referred to as "Out of Africa I." Marco

Langbroek, 'Out of Africa': An Investigation into the Earliest Occupation of the Old World (Oxford: Archaeopress, 2004). See also John G. Fleagle et al., Out of Africa I: The First Hominin Colonization of Eurasia (Stony Brook, NY: Springer Science and Business Media, 2010).

21. The Chimpanzee Sequencing and Analysis Consortium 2005 calculated the divergence between humans and chimpanzees at ~1.06 percent or less. See the Chimpanzee Sequencing and Analysis Consortium, "Initial Sequence of the Chimpanzee Genome and Comparison with the Human Genome," Nature 437, no. 7055 (2005): 69–87, https://www.nature.com/articles/nature04072. This similarity applies specifically to amino acid sequences, with almost a third identical and the rest different by only two amino acids. See Ajit Varki and Tasha K. Altheide, "Comparing the Human and Chimpanzee Genomes: Searching for Needles in a Haystack," Genome Research 15, no. 12 (2005): 1746–58, https://pubmed.ncbi.nlm.nih.gov/16339373/.

22. Homo erectus is credited with being the first hominin to exhibit extensive range expansion beyond Africa. While it is difficult to provide a single, precise timeline for their migration, fossil evidence shows that they spread to Java, Indonesia ("Java Man"), Northern China ("Peking Man"), Western Eurasia, and Europe, including England. See Susan C. Antón et al., "Morphological Variation in Homo erectus and the Origins of Developmental Plasticity," Philosophical Transactions of the Royal Society of London B 371, no. 1698 (July 2016): 20150236, https://royalsocietypublishing.org/doi/10.1098/rstb.2015.0236.

23. The University of California San Diego has a helpful overview of the ice ages on their CalSpace website Climate Change: Past and Future. See "Climate Change: Past and Future—The Ice Ages," CalSpace UCSD, http://earthguide.ucsd.edu/virtualmuseum/climatechange2/01_1.shtml.

24. The discoveries of eighty-thousand-year-old perforated shell beads at various inland sites in Morocco and at the Blombos Cave site, three hundred kilometers east of Cape Town, Africa, suggest that early humans were wearing and trading jewelry much earlier than previously thought. Paleoanthropologists now believe symbolic communication and modern human behavior developed earlier and more gradually throughout the Middle Paleolithic. See European Science Foundation, "Tiny Ancient Shells—80,000 Years Old—Point to Earliest Fashion Trend," Science Daily, August 27, 2009, https://www.sciencedaily.com/releases/2009/08/090827101204.htm. See also Abdeljalil Bouzouggar et al., "82,000-Year-Old Shell Beads from North Africa and Implications for the Origins of Modern Human Behavior," Proceedings of the National Academy of Sciences 104, no. 24 (2007): 9964–69, https://www.pnas.org/doi/full/10.1073/pnas.0703877104.

25. Clarkson et al. redated artifacts found earlier at Madjedbebe, Australia, using advanced techniques more powerful than radiocarbon dating. They determined that human occupation of Australia likely occurred more than sixty-five thousand years ago, setting a new minimum age for the arrival of humans in Australia. Their research established that these early Australians had a full complement of advanced Stone Age technology. See Chris Clarkson et al., "Human Occupation of Northern Australia by 65,000 Years Ago," Nature 547, no. 7663 (2017): 306–10, https://www.nature.com/articles/nature22968. Also of interest is Curtis W. Marean, "Early Signs of Human Presence in Australia," Nature 547, no. 7663 (2017): 285–86, https://www.nature.com/articles/547285a.

26. Pierre Teilhard de Chardin believed that the cerebralization process is characteristic of the universe as it progresses toward ever-more complex entities with increasing consciousness. He called this the law of "complexity-consciousness": that "whatever instance we may think of, we may be sure that every time a richer and better-organized structure will correspond to the more developed consciousness." The scale of complexity runs from atoms to the human, so the scale of consciousness also begins in the most rudimentary matter. He insists, "We are logically forced to assume the existence in rudimentary form ... of some sort of psyche in every corpuscle, even in those whose complexity is of such low or modest order as to render it imperceptible." Teilhard saw the development of cerebralization as a reflection of the universe's underlying spiritual energy, which he called the "Omega Point." According to Teilhard, this energy drives the universe toward greater complexity and consciousness, and humans have a role to play in this process. Pierre Teilhard de Chardin, *The Phenomenon of Man* (New York: Harper and Row, 1959), 60, 301–2. See also note 98.

27. The evolution of nervous systems was a gradual process, and pinpointing the first occurrence of a "brain" is challenging due to the nature of the fossil record and the definitions of what constitutes a brain. Fairly recently, an explosion of research on remarkably well-preserved fossil specimens from the Chengjiang fossil beds in Yunnan, China, is shifting our understanding of the evolutionary timeline of complex brains. In 2012, a complex brain structure connected to eyes and front appendages was identified in a 520-million-year-old fossil specimen of *Alalcomenaeus*, a now-extinct "great appendage" arthropod resembling a modern-day scorpion. See Gengo Tanaka et al., "Chelicerate Neural Ground Pattern in a Cambrian Great Appendage Arthropod," *Nature* 502, no. 7471 (2013): 364–67, https://www.nature.com/articles/nature12520. A year earlier, actual brain tissue from another 520-million-year-old arthropod called *Fuxianhuia protensa* was found in the same area. See Xiaoya Ma et al., "Complex Brain and Optic Lobes in an Early Cambrian Arthropod," *Nature* 490, no. 7419 (2012): 258–61, https://www.nature.com/articles/nature11495. Even more remarkable, in 2022, Strausfeld and Hirth described the structure of a brain in a wormlike creature with no head, called *Cardiodictyon catenulum*, also found in the Chengjiang deposits. Their finding suggests that the brain was already divided into three separate cerebral components before the evolution of the head. See Nicholas J. Strausfeld et al., "The Lower Cambrian Lobopodian Cardiodictyon Resolves the Origin of Euarthropod Brains," *Science* 378, no. 6622 (2022): 905–9, https://www.science.org/doi/10.1126/science.abn6264.

28. The sea jelly, also known as jellyfish, is a soft-bodied marine animal of the phylum *Cnidaria*, which includes jellyfish, corals, and sea anemones. *Cnidaria* does not have a centralized nervous system or a brain, but rather a decentralized network of nerve cells called a "nerve net." This type of nervous system is thought to be an ancient evolutionary adaptation that allowed the sea jelly to coordinate its movements and respond to environmental cues before the development of centralized brains in animals. One of the earliest animals to develop a nervous system is the phylum *Ctenophora*, or comb jellies, long believed to be a sister lineage to the sea jelly, forming the clade known as *Coelenterata*. However, recent research finds that the two lineages—*Cnidaria* and *Ctenophora*—are very dissimilar, challenging the sister lineage hypothesis. For a fascinating summary of research that supports convergent evolution of neural systems in the comb jelly and sea jelly lineages, see Leonid L. Moroz, "Convergent Evolution of Neural Systems in Ctenophores," *The Journal of Experimental Biology* 218, no. 4 (2015): 598–611, https://journals.biologists.

com/jeb/article/218/4/598/14147/Convergent-evolution-of-neural-systems-in. For an account of how modeling is helping contemporary researchers in neuroscience understand how neural activity leads to behavior in the jellyfish, see Fabian Pallasdies et al., "From Single Neurons to Behavior in the Jellyfish *Aurelia aurita*," *eLife* (2019): e50084, https:// elifesciences.org/articles/50084. See also note 118.

29. As global communication and interconnectivity increase, a growing sense of collective identity and shared human experience surpasses traditional boundaries like nationality. The efforts of organizations such as the Red Cross span across borders to provide relief in emergencies, while Doctors Without Borders, irrespective of national and cultural boundaries, delivers medical aid to alleviate human suffering. The scientific project is one of the most profound examples of global cooperation that transcends borders and cultures. The quest to uncover the truths of our universe is simply more important to scientists than their nationality.

30. In the three-story framework that the Human Energy project has developed to differentiate three types of worldviews, the first and second stories are deeply in opposition, and neither appreciates sufficiently the reality of time and the fact that the universe is a developing story. Only the *Third Story* sees the whole universe as a story of unfinished development and emerging relationships, in which deeper meaning and purpose are always dawning as "front" meets "future." See Human Energy, "The Three Stories of the Universe," https://humanenergy.io/the-three-stories-of-the-universe. See also note 6.

31. The process of evolution is almost always gradual, often involving numerous small changes that accumulate over time. The diversification of a single species or a small group of species into several different species, each adapted to fit a specific ecological niche, is called "adaptive radiation." Adaptive radiation, through the accumulation of small evolutionary changes, showcases the power of natural selection of genetic variation in driving biodiversity, especially in environments with diverse ecological opportunities. Eventually, the cumulative changes can become so pronounced that the populations become distinct species, unable to interbreed even if they were to come into contact. The classic example of adaptive radiation is the diversification of Darwin's finches on the Galápagos Islands. Darwin observed that these birds had a range of beak shapes and sizes, each specialized for a different food source, such as seeds, insects, or cacti. Over time, the finches evolved into multiple distinct species. It should be noted that speciation is not always a slow process. Rosemary and Peter Grant have recently documented interbreeding between a cross-island migrant finch and a native finch species, resulting in reproductive isolation and speciation in just two generations. See Sangeet Lamichhaney et al., "Rapid Hybrid Speciation in Darwin's Finches," *Science* 359, no. 6372 (2018): 224–28, https:// pubmed.ncbi.nlm.nih.gov/29170277/.

32. Fossil records dating back 225 million years reveal that *Brasilodon quadrangularis* had two sets of teeth, characteristic of extant mammals, not reptiles. This recent discovery suggests that *Brasilodon quadrangularis* and not the 210-million-year-old *Morganucodontids* is the earliest ancestor of all mammals. Both mammals are small, shrewlike animals measuring ten to twenty centimeters in length. See Sergio F. Cabreira et al., "Diphyodont Tooth Replacement of *Brasilodon*—A Late Triassic Eucynodont That Challenges the Time of

Origin of Mammals," *Journal of Anatomy* 241, no. 6 (2022): 1424–40, https://onlinelibrary.wiley.com/doi/abs/10.1111/joa.13756.

33. *Homo* is the genus popularly thought to have emerged from *Australopithecus* sometime between 2 and 2.5 million years ago. There are believed to be at least eight other human species apart from *Homo sapiens: habilis, erectus, rudolfensis, heidelbergensis, floresiensis, neanderthalensis, naledi* (discovered in 2015), and *luzonensis* (first found in 2019). There are considerable uncertainties present in this understanding, and the reevaluation of the phylogenetic tree for the genus *Homo* is the subject of ongoing research. See William H. Kimbel and Brian Villmoare, "From *Australopithecus* to *Homo*: The Transition That Wasn't," *Philosophical Transactions of the Royal Society B* 371, no. 1698 (July 2016), https://royalsocietypublishing.org/doi/10.1098/rstb.2015.0248.

34. It has long been believed that Hawaii was initially settled between 100 and 200 CE by travelers from the Island groups known as the Marquesas and the Society, both descendants of Austronesians who had sailed eastward from Southeast Asia approximately two thousand years earlier. This model understands New Zealand as having been colonized one thousand years later. However, anthropologists have recently advanced a new model based upon precise radiocarbon dating that "suggests this oceanic dispersal was far more rapid and recent than previously understood." See Philippa Mein Smith, *A Concise History of New Zealand*, 2nd ed. (New York: Cambridge University Press, 2012), 7–10.

35. The advent of agriculture in the Neolithic Era fundamentally changed the trajectory of human development. As hunter-gatherers shifted to farming, they no longer had to move about in search of food, leading to permanent settlements with growing populations. With the establishment of settled communities, complex societal structures with specialized roles, trade networks, significant technological innovation, and nature-based religious practices and ceremonies emerged. Jared Diamond has written a fascinating account of how agriculture's spread was facilitated by the physical migration of farming communities into new areas and the exchange of knowledge between different groups. Jared Diamond, *Gun, Germs, and Steel: The Fates of Human Societies* (New York: W. W. Norton & Company, 1999).

36. Taiz and Taiz have written a fascinating and brilliantly researched account of what human beings have thought about the lives of plants, particularly the sex lives of plants, throughout the eras of human history. They argue that it would not be until the end of the seventeenth century that sexuality in plants was discovered, even as the Mesopotamians first learned the technique of artificial pollination of date palms as early as the fifth millennium BCE. They point out,

> This delay is all the more remarkable when one considers that sex in animals was probably discovered around 14,000 years ago, when dogs were first domesticated and bred. Thus a span of more than 13,000 years separates the discovery of sex in animals and plants, even though humans have depended on plants and agriculture for their survival for at least 10,000 years. Equally astonishing, after the new sexual theory was first proposed by the British physician Nehemiah Grew in 1684, it was summarily rejected by some of the leading botanical lights of the day, and it continued to be challenged on philosophical, moral, and religious grounds for another 150 years until the middle of the nineteenth century!

Lincoln Taiz and Lee Taiz, *Flora Unveiled: The Discovery and Denial of Sex in Plants* (New York: Oxford University Press, 2017), 95, 3.

37. The myths of Inanna date to 3500 BCE or earlier and emphasize her close connection to crops, vegetation, and fertility. For an analysis of *The Courtship of Inanna and Dumuzi*; *Gilgamesh, Enkidu, and the Netherworld*; and *Inanna and Shukaletuda*, see Taiz and Taiz, *Flora Unveiled*, 85–137.

38. Taiz and Taiz, *Flora Unveiled*, 107–9.

39. The average number of organisms in one cubic centimeter of soil, as reported by Chandra, Srivastava, and Sharma, is ninety million bacteria, four million actinomycetes, two hundred thousand fungi, thirty thousand algae, five thousand protozoa, thirty nematodes, and less than one earthworm. These numbers provide a glimpse into the incredible microbial diversity and abundance of fertile soils, emphasizing the importance of soil health in agriculture and ecology. See Dinesh Chandra, Rashmi Srivastava, and A. K. Sharma, "Environment Friendly Phosphorus Biofertilizer as an Alternative to Chemical Fertilizers," in Bikas R. Pati and Santi M. Mandal, eds., *Recent Trends in Biofertilizers* (New Delhi: I. K. International, 2016), 43–71, https://www.researchgate.net/publication/291345421_Environment_friendly_Phosphorus_Biofertilizer_as_an_Alternative_to_Chemical_Fertilizers.

40. The estimated number of potentially habitable planets in the Milky Way galaxy is changing with emerging knowledge. Some studies estimate only about three hundred million Earth-like planets in our galaxy. See the webpage "How Many Earth-Like Planets Are There in the Universe," accessed October 20, 2021, https://www.bbvaopenmind.com/en/science/physics/how-many-earth-like-planets-are-in-the-universe-video-infographic/. Kunimoto and Matthews from the University of British Columbia, however, calculate six billion. See Michelle Kunimoto and Jaymie M. Matthews, "Searching the Entirety of Kepler Data. II. Occurrence Rate Estimates for FGK Stars," *The Astronomical Journal* 159, no. 6 (2020), https://iopscience.iop.org/article/10.3847/1538-3881/ab88b0/meta.

41. Drawing upon decades of scientific and engineering research, Mike Pitts explores the long-standing mystery of how Stonehenge was constructed. Mike Pitts, *How to Build Stonehenge* (London: Thames and Hudson Limited, 2022).

42. See Catherine Boeckmann, "Curious Ways Our Ancestors Tracked the Seasons," Almanac, January 9, 2024, https://www.almanac.com/content/ancient-sites-aligned-solstice-and-equinox.

43. Our readers in the northern hemisphere know that the summer solstice is the first day of summer and the longest day of the year. It may be less well known that the summer solstice occurs when the sun travels its highest path on the horizon, directly overhead above the Tropic of Cancer, located at 23.5° latitude north. For geographic locations at 23.5° latitude north, including parts of Mexico, the Bahamas, Egypt, Saudi Arabia, India, and southern China, the zenith sun of the summer solstice casts no shadows. It perhaps is no surprise that Earth's earliest astronomical site has been discovered in a culture near the tropics. The Nabta Playa in southern Egypt, discovered in the early 1990s by archaeologist Fred Wendorf, is close to 23.5° latitude north. Seven thousand years ago, cattle-worshiping nomads erected

massive stones that lined up with the path of the solstice sun, predating Stonehenge by almost two thousand years. See "Nabta Playa: Is The World's Oldest Astronomical Site Found in Africa?," *The Archaeologist*, December 16, 2021, https://www.thearchaeologist.org/blog/nabta-playa-is-the-worlds-oldest-astronomical-site-found-in-africa.

44. French Jesuit priest and paleontologist Pierre Teilhard de Chardin was among the first to recognize the developmental movement of the universe in time. His vision of cosmic evolution through its first two transformations is expressed in the first two books of *The Phenomenon of Man* (1959), first published in French in 1955. Swimme and Berry contrast the evolutionary perspective of developmental time with the cyclical notion of time characteristic of earlier views:

> The most significant change in the twentieth century, it seems, is our passage from a sense of cosmos to a sense of cosmogenesis. From the beginning of human consciousness, the ever-renewing seasonal sequence, with its death and rebirth cycles, has impinged most powerfully upon human thought. This orientation in consciousness has characterized every previous human culture up to our own. During the modern period, and especially in the twentieth century, we have moved from that dominant spatial mode of consciousness, where time is experienced in ever-renewing seasonal cycles, to a dominant time-developmental mode of consciousness, where time is experienced as an evolutionary sequence of irreversible transformations.

Brian Swimme and Thomas Berry, *The Universe Story: From the Primordial Flaring Forth to the Ecozoic Era—A Celebration of the Unfolding of the Cosmos* (New York: Harper, 1992), 2–3.

45. Artist scholars devoted to the work of activating time-developmental consciousness include Jennifer Morgan (see her trilogy for children: *Born with a Bang: The Universe Tells Our Cosmic Story; From Lava to Life: The Universe Tells Our Earth Story; and Mammals Who Morph: The Universe Tells Our Evolution Story*, illustrated by Dana Lynne Andersen (Nevada City, CA: Dawn Publications, 2002, 2003, and 2006, respectively); Blanche Marie Gallagher, BVM, *Homage to Teilhard: Visual Response*, http://libblogs.luc.edu/wla/2022/03/01/an-unexpected-journey-the-dreams-art-and-spirituality-of-sister-blanche-marie-gallagher-bvm/); and Mary C. Coehlo, "The New Origin Story," February 2014, https://vimeo.com/87299728.

46. In the video series *Canticle to the Cosmos*, Brian Thomas Swimme explores the way the universe develops through a series of irreversible onetime events. See Swimme's lecture "Episode 10: The Timing of Creativity," Center for the Story of the Universe, https://storyoftheuniverse.org/videos/canticle-to-the-cosmos/.

47. Wolfgang Leidhold has brilliantly detailed a series of nine transformations human experience has undergone from deep human history to today. The first is conscious sense perception, followed by the turn to imagination in the Paleolithic, then a sense of order, self-reflection, the eye of reason, spiritual experience, creativity, consciousness, and finally, according to Leidhold, the discovery of the unconscious. Key to his analysis is the view that the structure of human experience is not a universal constant but evolves over time. Leidhold, *The History of Experience.*

48. Memory is a fundamental aspect of existence, extending beyond human cognition to the physical properties of matter. Materials retain traces of their previous states, interactions, and processing history. This is evident in the phenomena of hysteresis, first observed and described in the context of magnetic materials by Sir James Alfred Ewing, an English physicist and engineer. The behavior of matter depends not only on current input and stimulus, but also on the path it has taken to arrive at its present moment. James A. Ewing, "On the Production of Transient Electric Currents in Iron and Steel Conductors by Twisting Them When Magnetized or by Magnetizing Them When Twisted," *Proceedings of the Royal Society of London* 33 (1881): 21–23.

49. Cytochrome c is a protein found in the mitochondria of cells, specifically in the electron transport chain, where it plays a crucial role in the production of energy. It is involved in the transfer of electrons between different components of the electron transport chain, ultimately leading to the building of ATP, the energy currency of the cell. A comprehensive overview of molecular biology and topics related to DNA, gene expression, and protein synthesis is provided by the definitive text Bruce Alberts et al., *Molecular Biology of the Cell* (New York: W. W. Norton & Company, 2022).

50. Migratory birds have the remarkable ability to navigate over tens of thousands of miles with an accuracy that is unattainable by human navigators. "To do so, they use their brains," says Professor Henrik Mouritsen, a leading researcher in the field of avian navigation and migratory behavior. For a fascinating article on how birds navigate using cues from their environment that they have learned to remember, including not only coastlines, rivers, mountain ranges, and the position of the sun and stars, but also the inclination, intensity, and direction of Earth's magnetic field, perceived with specialized magnetoreceptive systems, see Henrik Mouritsen, Dominik Heyers, and Onur Güntürkün, "The Neural Basis of Long-Distance Navigation in Birds," *Annual Review of Physiology* 78 (2016): 133–54, https://doi.org/10.1146/annurev-physiol-021115-10505.

51. Wolfgang Leidhold understands the various aspects of Paleolithic art as a deliberate, systematic method for evoking the reproductive imagination. He compares the Paleolithic human's development to that of a human child. Reproductive imagination is not yet active in a human infant but must be evoked. He asserts, "Since the human brain already has the imaginative potential, similar to the talent for speaking, it only needs to be stimulated to activate the power of the imagination. Just as the speech of adults makes children speak and learn a concrete language at the same time, training the imagination starts by necessitating its use." Leidhold, *The History of Experience*, 42–52.

52. Pierre Teilhard de Chardin writes, "The significance and biological function of the tool separated from the limb ... develops a kind of autonomous vitality. We have passive machines giving birth to the active machine, which in turn is followed by the automatic machine. Those are the main classifications, but within each classification what an immense proliferation there is of branches and offshoots, each endowed with a sort of evolutionary potential, irresistible both logically and biologically! We have only to think of the motorcar or the airplane." And what explains everything for Teilhard "is the extent to which this process of mechanization is a collective affair, and the way in which it finally creates, on the periphery of the human race, an organism that is collective in its

nature and amplitude." Pierre Teilhard de Chardin, *The Future of Man* (New York: Harper & Row, 1964), 164–65.

53. Thomas Berry understands the universe as having three key goals or purposes. The first aim encompasses the physical structure and organization of the universe, giving rise to galaxies and stars. The second aim is the development of life and species diversity, which includes the evolution of biological complexity and the emergence of consciousness. The third aim is the evolution of human awareness and the construction of communities. This aim encompasses the cultural, social, and spiritual dimensions of human life, including the development of language, art, religion, and ethics. It also entails the creation of social structures that foster the flourishing of life and promote the well-being of all entities. Thomas Berry, "Our Way into the Future," in *Dream of the Earth* (San Francisco: Sierra Club Books, 1990), 194–215.

54. Our understanding of Kalapalo culture is informed by the research of anthropologist Ellen Basso, as reported by Robert N. Bellah. Basso conducted fieldwork among the Kalapalo people, resulting in several influential publications that provide a detailed ethnographic account of Kalapalo social organization, kinship, and cosmology. The Kalapalo are an Indigenous tribe that live in the Upper Xingu region of central Brazil. They are part of the larger group of Indigenous peoples known as the Xinguano, who inhabit the southern part of the Amazon Basin. See Ellen B. Basso, *The Kalapalo Indians of Central Brazil* (New York: Holt, Rinehart, and Winston, 1973); and Basso, *A Musical View of the Universe: Kalapalo Myth and Ritual Performances* (Philadelphia: University of Pennsylvania Press, 1985). Robert N. Bellah, *Religion in Human Evolution: From the Paleolithic to the Axial Age* (Cambridge, MA: Belknap Press of Harvard University Press, 2011), 138–46.

55. As discussed in Chapter 4 of the Neolithic section, the construction of communities happens at every level of cosmic development: "Scattered atoms are brought together into the community of a star. Immense numbers of stars are drawn together into the community of the galaxy. On Earth, individual cells are woven into the multicellular community of a tree or an animal."

56. See Nick Gromicko, CMI, and Kenton Shepard, "The History of Concrete," the website for the International Association of Certified Home Inspectors, Inc., accessed May 11, 2023, https://www.nachi.org/history-of-concrete.htm. See also BigRentz, "The History of Concrete From Prehistory to Modern Times," 2023, https://www.bigrentz.com/blog/the-history-of-concrete.

57. See Ira Spar, "The Origins of Writing," in *Heilbrunn Timeline of Art History* (New York: The Metropolitan Museum of Art, 2004), http://www.metmuseum.org/toah/hd/wrtg/hd_wrtg.htm. See also Denise Schmandt-Besserat, "The Evolution of Writing," in James Wright, ed., *International Encyclopedia of Social and Behavioral Sciences* (Amsterdam: Elsevier, 2014), 16619–25.

58. Whether a star will "light up" involves a critical balance between gravity and fusion. A minimum number of atoms condensing under the force of gravity is required to reach the necessary core temperature for hydrogen fusion. Once initiated, fusion-driven outward pressure counterbalances the star's inward gravitational pull, creating an equilibrium

and maintaining its stability during its main sequence phase. The mass of our sun is 1.99×10^{30} kilograms. Given that the mass of a hydrogen atom is approximately 1.67×10^{-27} kilograms, the number of hydrogen atoms needed to light our sun is found by dividing the hydrogen mass of the sun by the mass of a hydrogen atom: $(1.99 \times 10^{30} \text{ kg}) / (1.67 \times 10^{-27} \text{ kg/hydrogen atom}) = 1.19 \times 10^{57}$ hydrogen atoms. Astronomers calculate that the minimum mass of gas needed to generate core temperatures high enough to begin nuclear fusion is about .08 times the mass of our sun, or 1.59×10^{29} kg. Thus, the minimum number of atoms in close proximity necessary to light even the smallest star is $(1.59 \times 10^{29} \text{ kg}) / (1.67 \times 10^{-27} \text{ kg/hydrogen atom}) = 9.5 \times 10^{55}$ hydrogen atoms. Gas cloud formations with populations less than 9.5×10^{55} hydrogen atoms are too small to become stars. Pressure and gravity enter equilibrium before the core temperature rises enough to fuse hydrogen. These "protostars" eventually cool and become "brown dwarfs." Astronomers believe "up to 100 billion cold, dark, brown dwarfs may lurk in the depths of interstellar space, comparable to the total number of 'real' stars in our galaxy." Eric Chaisson and Steve McMillan, *Astronomy: A Beginner's Guide to the Universe*, 4th ed. (Upper Saddle River, NJ: Pearson Education, 2004), 241, 306–7.

59. See Mélanie Roffet-Salque et al., "Widespread Exploitation of the Honeybee by Early Neolithic Farmers, *Nature* 527 (November 2015): 226–30, https://www.nature.com/articles/nature15757. See also American Ceramic Society, "A Brief History of Ceramics and Glass," accessed May 11, 2023, https://ceramics.org/about/what-are-engineered-ceramics-and-glass/brief-history-of-ceramics-and-glass.

60. In the video series *Canticle to the Cosmos*, Brian Thomas Swimme elaborates on the concept of "noble enemies" using the hawk and mouse as an example of how the dynamic interplay of seemingly opposing forces can be part of an extended creative process that ultimately leads to greater complexity and diversity. See Swimme's lecture "Episode 5: Destruction and Loss," Center for the Story of the Universe, https://storyoftheuniverse.org/videos/canticle-to-the-cosmos/.

61. We have seen this dynamic before. The supernova must spread its elements in order for their potencies to be actualized. The dispersal of elements in a time-developing universe is essential for actualizing creative potencies.

62. Intelligence is generally understood to involve both general problem-solving skills and the ability to apply a particular expertise acquired from the practice of specific skills. Raymond Cattell distinguishes between what he calls "fluid intelligence" and "crystallized intelligence." Fluid intelligence involves the power of concentration, thought, reasoning, the ability to perceive relationships, and the aptitude for solving unfamiliar problems. Crystallized intelligence is understood to be derivative of general fluid intelligence and consists of skills and knowledge refined by education, culture, and experience. Howard Gardner's theory of multiple intelligences departs from this understanding of general intelligence and argues for multiple unrelated forms of intelligence, including linguistic, musical, logical and mathematical, spatial, systematic, kinesthetic, self-awareness and control, and sensitivity to social signals. Gardner argues that distinct abilities are not derived from general intelligence and would not be found to correlate in intelligence testing if pure forms of each type of intelligence could be tested. James W. Kalat, *Introduction to Psychology*, 11th ed. (Boston: Cengage Learning, 2017), 289–92.

63. Chimpanzees have been found not only to make tools but to use those tools systematically and consistently for hunting. See Jill D. Pruetz and Paco Bertolani, "Savanna Chimpanzees, *Pan troglodytes verus*, Hunt with Tools," *Current Biology* 17 (March 6, 2007): 412–17. We should not be surprised, then, by recent evidence suggesting that human use of spear tips for hunting predates both *Homo sapiens* and Neanderthals to their last common ancestor, *Homo heidelbergensis*. Five-hundred-thousand-year-old spear points used for hunting have been recovered from the archaeological site of Kathu Pan in South Africa. See Jayne Wilkins et al., "Evidence for Early Hafted Hunting Technology," *Science* 338, no. 6109 (2012): 942–46, https://pubmed.ncbi.nlm.nih.gov/23161998/.

64. Bison jump sites occur in the archaeological record throughout North America, from "Head Smashed-In" Buffalo Jump in Alberta, Canada, around five thousand years ago to possibly the oldest known site at "Bonfire Shelter" in Texas (10,230 +/– 160 BP). For a comparison of the buffalo jumps throughout North America and a discussion of the development and function of this complex hunting method, see Kristen Carlson and Leland Bement, "Organization of Bison Hunting at the Pleistocene/Holocene Transition on the Plains of North America," *Quaternary International* 297 (2013): 93–99.

65. Domestication, distinct from management and agriculture, is a coevolutionary mutualistic relationship between domesticator and domesticate. For an understanding of core concepts in domestication research and a scientific discussion of the profound and lasting global impacts of domestication of animals and plants, see Melinda A. Zeder, "Core Questions in Domestication Research," *Proceedings of the National Academy of Sciences* 112, no. 11 (2015): 3191–98.

66. The Gaia hypothesis was initially advanced to account for the long-term stability of Earth's environment for life despite increasing solar luminosity. The Gaia hypothesis postulates that "the ensemble of living organisms which constitute the biosphere might act as a single entity to regulate chemical composition, surface pH, and possibly climate." See James Lovelock and Lynn Margulis, "Atmospheric Homeostasis by and for the Biosphere: The Gaia Hypothesis," *Tellus* 26 (1974): 3. Lovelock compared Gaia with a living, homeostatic entity, a kind of "mega-organism," but was careful to emphasize this was not to say Gaia was a sentient being. See James Lovelock, *Gaia: A New Look at Life on Earth* (Oxford: Oxford University Press, 2000), 12, xi. Lynn Margulis, too, objected to the widespread and unscientific personification of Gaia and emphasized that Gaia is not an organism but an emergent property of relations among organisms, the spherical planet, and the sun as an energy source. See Lynn Margulis, *Symbiotic Planet: A New View of Evolution* (New York: Basic Books, 1998).

67. Humans have been called the "world's greatest evolutionary force," frequently driving both extinction and speciation. See S. R. Palumbi, "Humans as the World's Greatest Evolutionary Force," *Science* 293, no. 5536 (2001): 1786–90, https://www.science.org/doi/abs/10.1126/science.293.5536.1786. For consideration and comparison of how human influences are shaping evolution across a full range of contexts, see Andrew P. Hendry, Kiyoko M. Gotanda, and Erik I. Svensson, "Human Influences on Evolution, and the Ecological and Societal Consequences," *Philosophical Transactions of the Royal Society B* 372, no. 1712 (January 2017): 20160028, https://royalsocietypublishing.org/doi/10.1098/rstb.2016.0028.

68. Brian Thomas Swimme discusses synergy as one of the fundamental creative principles of the universe leading to the emergence of increasingly complex forms of matter and consciousness in his video series *Powers of the Universe*. Swimme argues that the universe is constantly evolving through the process of synergy and that human beings have the potential to participate in this creative process by working together in harmonious and collaborative ways. See Swimme's lecture "Episode 7: Synergy," Center for the Story of the Universe, https://storyoftheuniverse.org/power-of-the-universe/.

69. The lifetime of a free-floating neutron has been calculated at 14.629 minutes +/− 0.005 minutes. See F. M. Gonzalez et al., "Improved Neutron Lifetime Measurement with UCNτ," *Physical Review Letters* 127, no. 162501 (October 13, 2021), https://journals.aps.org/prl/abstract/10.1103/PhysRevLett.127.162501.

70. British physicist James Chadwick won the 1935 Nobel Prize in Physics for discovering the neutron, which provided the missing piece in understanding atomic structure. With his discovery, it became clear that atomic nuclei consisted of both protons and neutrons and that the electrons orbited the nucleus. This also clarified why atomic masses were higher than atomic numbers since neutrons contribute to the mass of an atom but not the charge. Because a neutron is electrically neutral, it must be bound into the atomic nucleus by a force independent of electric charge; this is the so-called strong nuclear force. The neutron is stable within a nucleus but unstable in a free state. The neutron's slow decay indicates yet another nuclear force called the weak force. See James Chadwick, "The Possible Existence of a Neutron," *Nature* 129, no. 3252 (1932): 312.

71. Lab measurements of lunar rock collected by the Apollo missions to the moon and terrestrial rocks of Earth reveal that the moon's minerals are virtually indistinguishable from the Earth for nearly every isotopic system. This finding has presented a challenge to the prevailing theory of the moon's formation that hypothesizes a collision between the newly accreted Earth and a Mars-sized planet named "Theia." If the "Giant Impact Theory" is true, the moon's composition should include significant material from both Theia and Earth. Interestingly, more recent studies have revealed that deeper into the moon's mantle and at its core, the isotopic composition of the moon is distinct from Earth, possibly preserving a postimpact Theia-like composition. See Erick J. Cano, Zachary D. Sharp, and Charles K. Shearer, "Distinct Oxygen Isotope Compositions of the Earth and Moon," *Nature Geoscience* 13, no. 4 (2020): 270–74, https://www.nature.com/articles/s41561-020-0550-0. See also Sune G. Nielsen, David V. Bekaert, and Maureen Auro, "Isotopic Evidence for the Formation of the Moon in a Canonical Giant Impact," *Nature Communications* 12, no. 1 (2021): 1–7, https://www.nature.com/articles/s41467-021-22155-7.

72. Diatoms are microscopic algae found in oceans, freshwater bodies, and soils. Though tiny, their abundance gives them a critical role in global biogeochemical cycles, especially regarding oxygen production and carbon sequestration. Estimates suggest that diatoms produce between 20 and 40 percent of the Earth's oxygen and facilitate up to 25 percent of all organic carbon fixation occurring on Earth, comparable in both processes to the achievement of all the world's tropical rainforests combined. See Katherine M. Johnson, "The Air We Breathe, and the Water We Drink: Why Diatoms Are So Important," Phinizy Center for Water Sciences, accessed September 6, 2023,

https://phinizycenter.org/the-air-we-breathe-and-the-water-we-drink-why-diatoms-are-so-important/.

73. "Thinking about thinking" began with the emergence of a capacity for *theoria*, a contemplative way of looking *at* the world in what has been called the "axial age." Robert N. Bellah attributes the first use of the term *axial age* to the German philosopher Karl Jaspers. The term refers to the "spiritual process that occurred between 800 and 200 BCE," when, according to Jaspers, as quoted by Bellah, "Man, as we know him today, came into being." See Robert N. Bellah, *Religion in Human Evolution: From the Paleolithic to the Axial Age* (Cambridge: The Belknap Press of Harvard University Press, 2011), 268.

74. Contemporary philosopher, cognitive scientist, and neuroscientist Alva Noë criticizes present-day neuroscience's impoverished conception that brain mechanics can explain consciousness and thought. Consciousness is not in the confines of the brain, he argues, but also involves our bodies in dynamic relations with the world around us. See Alva Noë, *Out of Our Heads: Why You Are Not Your Brain and Other Lessons from the Biology of Consciousness* (New York: Hill and Wang, 2009).

75. Our use of the term "hyperbody" is drawn from the "hyperphysics" of Pierre Teilhard de Chardin. For Teilhard, the entire universe is oriented toward wholeness, increasingly complexified and increasingly conscious. Consciousness is interiority, underscoring matter in the direction of the future. Love is the fundamental nature of reality, embedded as the physical fabric of the universe. See Pierre Teilhard de Chardin, *Human Energy* (New York: Harcourt, 1962), 72. It is not a world of being in *extensia* but a world of relationships bringing matter into union. Being is not the primary ontological category; union is the primary ontological category. Teilhard calls his philosophical orientation "hyperphysics" because it is beyond a material understanding of the universe; he chooses the word "hyperphysics" instead of "metaphysics" because the subject matter is not above or beyond being, but *more* being in relational interdependence. See "Author's Note" in Teilhard de Chardin, *The Human Phenomenon* (Brighton: Sussex Academic Press, 1999), 1–2. See also note 130 in this volume.

76. Brian Thomas Swimme writes,

Looking out at the stars, we will imagine the vastness of a trillion galaxies and will know we are beholding that which constructed the eyes that are doing the beholding. Our minds will be challenged to make the figure-ground transformation: *the inner is looking at the outer, which has given birth to the inner.* . . . Though floating in space on a tiny planet, we are also the universe as a whole that has achieved its self-awareness.

Brian Thomas Swimme, *Cosmogenesis: An Unveiling of the Expanding Universe* (Berkeley, CA: Counterpoint, 2022), 315.

77. Teilhard de Chardin viewed existential depression and the belief that the universe is absurd as a crisis in human energy and sought ways to cultivate a "zest for life" in humankind. We are called to reimagine and reinvent the human, but only with energy can we rise to the task. Humankind is "conscious—dangerously and critically so—conscious and perfected

to the point of being able to control its own driving forces and to rebound upon itself. But what good would this great cosmic event be to us if we were *to lose the zest for evolution?*" Zest for evolution is the spiritual equivalent of a physical source of energy. Teilhard points out, "All over the earth the attention of thousands of engineers and economists is concentrated on the problem of world resources of coal, oil or uranium—and yet nobody, on the other hand, bothers to carry out a survey of the zest for life: to take its 'temperature,' to feed it, to look after it, and (why not, indeed?) to increase it." See Pierre Teilhard de Chardin, *Activation of Energy* (London: William Collins Sons & Co., 1970), 236–37.

78. Anatomically modern humans (*Homo sapiens*) emerged more than 300,000 years ago. The common understanding of scientists has placed the origin of *Homo sapiens* in sub-Saharan Africa some 200,000 years ago. See Rebecca L. Cann, Mark Stoneking, and Allan C. Wilson, "Mitochondrial DNA and Human Evolution," *Nature* 325, no. 6099 (1987): 31–36, https://www.nature.com/articles/325031a0. More recently, however, *Homo sapiens* remains dating to 315,000 years ago have been found in Morocco, suggesting *Homo sapiens* dispersed throughout the African continent more than 300,000 years ago. See Ewen Callaway, "Oldest *Homo sapiens* Fossil Claim Rewrites Our Species History," *Nature* (June 2017), https://www.nature.com/articles/nature.2017.22114.

79. Insects were the first animals to evolve wings and flight some 325 million years ago and are the only invertebrates to do so. Pterygota is the subclass of insects comprising 99.9 percent of all insects, including winged insects and all orders of flightless insects whose ancestors had wings. The hypothesis that wings capable of flight evolved from thoracic protrusions used as radiators is one of several hypotheses as to the origin of the insect wing. For a discussion of Pterygota, wings, and the evolution of flight, see Chapter 6, "Insects Take to the Skies," in David Grimaldi and Michael Engel, *Evolution of the Insects* (Cambridge: Cambridge University Press, 2005), 155–59.

80. Ken Burns has called the Dust Bowl "the greatest man-made ecological disaster in American history." *The Dust Bowl*, directed by Ken Burns (2012; PBS International, 2012), https://www.pbs.org/kenburns/the-dust-bowl/.

81. Diamandis and Kotler emphasize the importance of changing from a scarcity mindset to an abundance mindset. See Peter H. Diamandis and Steven Kotler, *Abundance: The Future Is Better Than You Think* (New York: Free Press, 2012). They argue that we are amid rapidly accelerating technological growth and that the convergence of accelerating technologies further fuels the rate of innovation and the possibility for transformative solutions. See Peter H. Diamandis and Steven Kotler, *The Future Is Faster Than You Think: How Converging Technologies Are Transforming Business, Industries, and Our Lives* (New York: Simon & Schuster, 2020).

82. Wolfgang Leidhold understands "the turn to self-reflection," or self-awareness, as a distinct mode of experience that occurs earlier than self-consciousness. He writes,

> Although ... the experience of participation has emerged since about the Mesolithic, participation in the self develops only later in the Bronze Age. Until then, attention to the pole of the experiencing person was still missing,

as knowledge originated in the sacred sphere, from where it was transferred as a ready-made product to the human side that remained a passive recipient of divine gifts. The transition from the role of the passive recipient to that of an active subject or author is the hallmark of the *turn to self-reflection*.

See Leidhold, *The History of Experience*, 88–89.

83. Zarathustra's words are paraphrased from *The Gathas of Zarathustra and the Other Old Avestan Texts* as quoted by Leidhold. See Wolfgang Leidhold, *The History of Experience*, 95.

84. "Leap in being" is a fundamental concept in Eric Voegelin's philosophy of history, used to describe transformative moments in the history of human consciousness and understanding. He speaks of the "leap in being" in volume I of *Order and History* as an actual change in being "with consequences for the order of existence." See Eric Voegelin, *Order and History*, 5 vols. (Baton Rouge: Louisiana State University Press, 1956–1987), 49. German Swiss psychiatrist and philosopher Karl Jaspers also spoke of humans experiencing a leap in spiritual and intellectual development across various civilizations during what is called the "axial age." See note 73.

85. The axial age began with the emergence of a capacity for *theoria* that differentiates the transcendent from the immanent, the universal from the particular, and the absolute from the contingent, and firmly entrenched humanity in a cosmology that has the human— uniquely ennobled with rationality and morality—in control of a mechanistic, material earth of inert matter. The human world—its science, religion, politics, economics, medicine, and education—is firmly entrenched in a metaphysics of being that emphasizes space and rationality over time and experience. The present authors speculate that time-developmental awareness may have the potential to spawn a transformation of consciousness, the significance of which might even parallel the axial emergence of the theoretical mind, called the tragic "leap in being" by Eric Voegelin. In our present moment, the leap in being is a "leap in becoming" beyond the isolated and internal rational mind to include a deep communion with the whole of the universe in relational developing time.

86. Denise Schmandt-Besserat, a French American archaeologist best known for her work on the history and invention of writing, has shown that the use of writing on tokens for economic purposes provided the impetus for developing early writing systems as early as 3400 BCE. Schmandt-Besserat proposes a direct link between administrative token use and the emergence of cuneiform writing and the Sumerian script. See Denise Schmandt-Besserat, "The Earliest Precursor of Writing," *Scientific American* 238 (1978): 50–59; "An Archaic Recording System and the Origin of Writing," *Syro-Mesopotamian Studies* 1, no. 2 (1977): 1–32.

87. The writing of odes, hymns, poetry, and myths emerged independently in different parts of the world, beginning around 2500 BCE. See Evan Andrews, *History* (A&E Television Networks, August 10, 2023), https://www.history.com/news/what-is-the-oldest-known-piece-of-literature. *She Who Wrote: Enheduanna and Women of Mesopotamia, ca. 3400–2000 B.C.* is a 2023 Morgan Library & Museum exhibition that highlights the writing of the ancient Mesopotamian poet and priestess Enheduanna, the first known nonanonymous author in world history. Enheduanna's temple hymns—that is,

incantations to the gods and goddesses of the Sumerian and the Akkadian Empires— were autobiographical and unitive, articulating the relatable challenges and insecurities of her personal experience and facilitating a tremendous boon to the exchange of ideas. Considered a pioneer of the "reflective turn" by philosopher Wolfgang Leidhold, Enheduanna's texts were used to teach writing in the scribal schools of ancient Mesopotamia for hundreds of years. See the Morgan Library and Museum, *She Who Wrote: Enheduanna and Women of Mesopotamia, ca. 3400–2000 B.C.*, The Morgan Library and Museum, New York, October 14, 2022–February 19, 2023, https://www.themorgan.org/exhibitions/she-who-wrote. See Leidhold, *The History of Experience*, 90–93.

88. Cyanobacteria were the first organisms to evolve oxygenic photosynthesis using chlorophyll a, the same primary pigment that modern plants use. The evolution of cyanobacteria and their oxygenic photosynthesis was a game-changing event in Earth's history because it dramatically increased the amount of oxygen in the atmosphere, leading to the Great Oxygenation Event around 2.3 billion years ago. It is worth noting that while cyanobacteria introduced the mechanism of oxygenic photosynthesis that dominates today, the chloroplasts in modern plants—where photosynthesis occurs—are believed to have originated from an ancestral cyanobacterium that was engulfed by a eukaryotic cell in a symbiotic relationship, a process called endosymbiosis. See Lars Olof Björn and Govindjee, "The Evolution of Photosynthesis and Chloroplasts," *Current Science* 96, no. 11 (2009): 1466–74.

89. Teilhard de Chardin describes "the 'front of the wave' carrying the world of man towards its new destiny." He says, "The front cannot but attract us, because it is, in one way, the *extreme boundary* between what one is already aware of, and what is still in process of formation"; at the front, "you seem to feel that you're at the final boundary between what has already been achieved and what is striving to emerge." See Pierre Teilhard de Chardin, *Heart of Matter* (New York: Harcourt, 1978), 167–68.

> I'm still in the same quiet billets. Our future continues to be pretty vague, both as to when and what it will be. What the future imposes on our present existence is not exactly a feeling of depression;—it's rather a sort of seriousness, of detachment, of a broadening, too, of outlook. This feeling, of course, borders on a sort of sadness (the sadness that accompanies every fundamental change); but it leads also to a sort of higher joy. I should be inclined to think that during these periods of waiting, a slow but continual process of adaptation is going on, at the end of which the soul finds that it has been raised up to the level of the great duties that await it.... I'd call it "Nostalgia for the Front." There is such a feeling without any doubt at all.... The reasons, I believe, come down to this; the front cannot but attract us, because it is, in one way, the *extreme boundary* between what one is already aware of, and what is still in process of formation. Not only does one see there things that you experience nowhere else, but one also sees emerge from within one an underlying stream of clarity, energy, and freedom that is to be found hardly anywhere else in ordinary life—and the new form that the soul then takes on is that of the individual living the quasi-collective life of all men, fulfilling a function far higher than that of the individual, and becoming fully conscious of this new state. It goes without saying that at the front you no longer look on things in the

same way as you do in the rear; if you did, the sights you see and the life you lead would be more than you could bear. This exaltation is accompanied by a certain pain. Nevertheless it is indeed an exaltation. And that's why one likes the front in spite of everything, and misses it.

See Teilhard de Chardin, *The Making of a Mind: Letters from a Soldier Priest [1914–1919]* (New York: Harper & Row, 1961), 205.

90. Priest, poet, and political revolutionary Ernesto Cardenal has hundreds of names for what we call "the extraordinary realm." See Ernesto Cardinal, *Cosmic Canticles* (Willimantic, CT: Curbstone Press, 1993).

91. Scientist Timothy E. Eastman articulates a "*Logoi* framework" that ascribes full "ontologically real" status to both potentiality and actuality in relational reality. He references the philosopher Randall E. Auxier:

"The actual and possible together effectively form what [Josiah] Royce means by the 'real,' and the order we hypothesize for those relations is the universally mediating relation of time. The 'possible' is associated with the future and the 'actual' with the past, while the present moment is an indefinite duration that links what is actual to what is possible in overlapping … nested hierarchies of time-spans." Randall E. Auxier, *Time, Will, and Purpose: Living Ideas from the Philosophy of Josiah Royce* (Chicago: Open Court, 2013), 59.

See Timothy E. Eastman, *Untying the Gordian Knot: Process, Reality, and Context* (Lanham, MD: Lexington Books, 2020), 23.

92. Astrobiologist Bruce Damer hypothesizes that life could only have come forth in land-based freshwater pools, challenging the long-held belief by origin-of-life scientists that life emerged in Earth's ocean. The dynamics of a molten earth showered with the radiant energy of the sun enabled minerals to construct a spherical membrane, a profound achievement that then enabled the creation of ever more complex molecules. Inside the stable organization of a membrane-protected sphere, the creativity of interacting molecules found a way to transform nonliving molecules into living cells. See Bruce F. Damer and David W. Deamer, "The Hot Spring Hypothesis for an Origin of Life," *Astrobiology* 20 (2020): 429–52, https://www.liebertpub.com/doi/full/10.1089/ast.2019.2045. Process philosopher Matthew David Segall works with Bruce Damer to dynamically integrate the metaphysical and empirical aspects of origin-of-life science. See Matthew David Segall and Bruce Damer, "The Cosmological Context of the Origin of Life: Process Philosophy and the Hot Spring Hypothesis," Footnotes2Plato.com, https://matthewsegall.files.wordpress.com/2022/10/final-draft-sept-25-2022-the-cosmological-context-of-the-origins-of-life.pdf.

93. See Susan Whitfield, "Alfalfa, Pasture and the Horse in China: A Review Article," *Quaderni di Studi Indo-Mediterranei* 12 (2020): 227–45.

94. Qin Shi Huang, the first emperor of the Qin Dynasty, pursued a vast militarist expansion policy that began in 230 BCE and culminated in the establishment of a single Chinese empire by 221 BCE, setting into place the necessary prerequisites for what would

later become the famous Silk Road trade route. He commissioned the construction of an extensive network of roads and canals throughout the empire, used for the movement of troops, goods, and communication. He endeavored to build a continuous defensive wall that connected and extended the walls of the former states to protect the newly unified empire from northern tribes, particularly the Xiongnu. The paramount achievement of the Qin Dynasty was the standardization of the nonalphabetic written script across six Zhou Dynasty states and the founding of a centralized academy to manage all textual content, supplanting existing regional scripts and facilitating faster and more concise communication between regions with different spoken languages. The Qin Dynasty also standardized weights and measures, forging bronze standards of measurement they disseminated to regional administrators who enforced their use by local merchants. While the establishment and growth of the Silk Road occurred during the Han Dynasty, which followed the Qin, Qin Shi Huang created a more unified, structured, and protected empire within which the trade routes of subsequent eras could flourish. See History.Com Editors, "Qin Dynasty," updated June 16, 2023, https://www.history.com/topics/ancient-china/qin-dynasty.

95. Around 210 BCE, Qin Shi Huang introduced a uniform round copper coin with a central hole in the middle and abolished all other forms of local currency. The body of these early coins was called their "flesh" (肉), and the central hole was known as "the good" (好). See Ulrich Theobald, "Huanqian 圜錢, Round Coins of the Warring States and the Qin Periods," *China Knowledge*, June 24, 2016, http://www.chinaknowledge.de/History/Terms/huanqian.html.

96. The concept of "critical density" involves a balance between opposing forces and operates in distinct contexts at every level of existence. In the context of the universe, two primary dynamics are at play: the expansion of the universe famously observed by Edwin Hubble in 1964 and the gravitational force of all matter and energy that counters the expansion. The critical density of the universe is the average density needed for its expansion to stop eventually. In the context of stars, the main forces are the inward gravitational pull that collapses the star and the outward pressure that results from nuclear fusion and thermal energy. For fusion to initiate in the core of a protostar, a specific critical density is required. See also note 58.

97. The energy stored as glucose in plants is used by animals like the cheetah, who effectively ingest that stored energy when they consume plants (or other animals who have eaten plants). The cheetah then uses this energy to fuel its activities, including running at high speeds. The transformation of chemical energy in glucose into kinetic energy in a moving cheetah is facilitated by the metabolic process called the citric acid cycle, otherwise known as the Krebs cycle, named after its discoverer, Sir Hans Adolf Krebs. See Bryan A. Wilson, Jonathan C. Schisler, and Monte S. Willis, "Sir Hans Adolf Krebs: Architect of Metabolic Cycles," *Laboratory Medicine* 41, no. 6 (June 2010): 377–380, https://academic.oup.com/labmed/article/41/6/377/2657667.

98. The noosphere can be thought of as a collective extension of humankind called the "hyperbody," giving rise to a shared experience. Just as tools are the bodylike aspect of the hyperbody, cerebralization is its mindlike aspect. See also notes 26, 75, and 130.

99. See P. A. M. Dirac, "Cosmological Models and the Large Numbers Hypothesis," *Proceedings of the Royal Society of London, Series A, Mathematical and Physical Sciences* 338, no. 1615 (1974): 439–46, http://www.jstor.org/stable/78591.

100. In the early 1970s, as part of a CBS documentary series entitled *Physics and Beyond*, Nobel Prize–winning physicist Paul Dirac was interviewed by F. David Peat and Paul Buckley about the occurrence of large number constants in physical theories and Dirac's contention that these numbers are interrelated and connected with the age of the universe. Transcripts of this interview and other conversations with leading scientists of the twentieth century can be found in Paul Buckley and F. David Peat, *Glimpsing Reality: Ideas in Physics and the Link to Biology* (London: Routledge, 2009).

101. An early publication by Bernard Carr, professor of mathematics and astronomy at Queen Mary University of London and president of the Scientific and Medical Network, and Martin Rees, another recognized expert on the early universe, highlights the puzzling fact that six different fundamental constants involving the large-scale structure of the universe and the microscopic world of particle physics seem to be "just right" for the existence of galaxies, life, and, ultimately, human conscious self-awareness to exist. This puzzling fact has been named the "Barr-Rees coincidence" or the "Goldilocks Enigma." See B. J. Carr and M. J. Rees, "The Anthropic Principle and the Structure of the Physical World," *Nature* 278 (1979): 605–12. The fact that the constants of nature are fine-tuned has led to various interpretations. Bernard Carr, in particular, has been a strong proponent of what has been called the "strong anthropic principle," arguing that the universe must have purpose and meaning beyond its physical laws and structures. See Bernard Carr, "The Anthropic Principle Revisited," in Bernard Carr, ed., *Universe or Multiverse?* (Cambridge: Cambridge University Press, 2007), 77–90.

102. *The Anthropic Cosmological Principle* is a rich and comprehensive exploration of the anthropic principle and its implications for our understanding of the universe. Barrow and Tipler argue that the Anthropic Cosmological Principle can be seen as a necessary consequence of the laws of nature and the universe's structure. They explore three different forms the principle can take: the Weak Anthropic Principle (WAP), the Strong Anthropic Principle (SAP), and the Final Anthropic Principle (FAP). The WAP states, "*The observed values of all physical and cosmological quantities are not equally probable, but they take on values restricted by the requirement that there exist sites where carbon-based life can evolve and by the requirement that the Universe be old enough for it to have already done so.*" A more assertive form of the principle is the SAP, which posits, "*The Universe must have those properties which allow life to develop within it at some stage in its history.*" The word "must" suggests a kind of necessity or purpose to the universe that seems to point toward design or destiny. Finally, the FAP is a more generalized form of the SAP, suggesting a sort of cosmic destiny for intelligence. The FAP states, "*Intelligent information-processing must come into existence in the Universe, and, once it comes into existence, it will never die out.*" The FAP is the most provocative of the principles outlined by Barrow and Tipler. See John D. Barrow and Frank J. Tipler, *The Anthropic Cosmological Principle* (New York: Oxford University Press, 1986), 16, 23.

103. Convergence is the force by which the noosphere rises and the universe experiences itself as a communion event in human consciousness. Teilhard de Chardin writes, "With and

since the coming of Man a new law of Nature has come into force—that of convergence. The convergence of the phyla both ensues from, and of itself leads to, the coming together of individuals.... And out of this convergence, as I have said, there arises a very real social inheritance, produced by the synthetic recording of human experience." See Teilhard de Chardin, *The Future of Man*, 165.

104. The process of uniting the existing walls into what is now referred to as the Great Wall of China was initiated by Emperor Qin Shi Huang, the first emperor of a unified China. He reigned from 221 BCE to 210 BCE after successfully consolidating power and uniting the various warring states into a single Chinese empire. See History.Com Editors, "Qin Dynasty," updated June 16, 2023, https://www.history.com/topics/ancient-china/qin-dynasty. For historical context, see also note 94.

105. The quoted words are from "The Western Inscription," written by Zhang Zai, a neo-Confucian philosopher who lived during the Sung Dynasty (960–1279). For Zhang Zai, the most essential principle of ethics is *ren*, which means benevolence or humanity in flourishing community. *Ren* is a moral principle that applies to the whole universe. See Chang Tsai, "The Western Inscription," in *A Source Book in Chinese Philosophy*, translated by Wing-Tsit Chan (Princeton, NJ: Princeton University Press, 1963), 497.

106. For additional information about the Parliament of the World's Religions events, see the Pluralism Project at www.pluralism.org. Based at Harvard University, the Pluralism Project is a research endeavor designed to comprehend the evolving nature of religious communities in the United States and to promote dialogue between individuals of various religious traditions. Regarding the first World Parliament of Religions held in Chicago in 1893, they state, "The predominant spirit of the three-week event was a kind of welcoming universalism or inclusivism on the part of the Western, mostly Christian, hosts. From every religion, however, speakers optimistically affirmed the universal principles that surely would undergird all faiths. The word 'universalism' tolled like a bell through the halls of the Parliament. The world stood on the technological brink of global civilization, and the hope for the universal in matters of the spirit was just beginning to be voiced." As regards the centennial event of 1993, which opened in the same city, they note the radical change that had occurred in the religious face of the United States: "By this time, America itself had become a truly multi-religious country and the Hindu, Buddhist, Christian, Muslim, Sikh, and Jewish organizers were residents of a very different Chicago."

107. American scientist Jared Diamond has written extensively on the subject of bio-cultural evolution. He argues that variations in the habitats of evolving human societies account for differences in technological and economic development. He contends that societies that had access to animals and plants that could be domesticated were more likely to develop complex technologies. See Diamond, *Guns, Germs, and Steel*. Terrence Deacon is an anthropologist who argues that the human brain and culture evolved together, shaping each other over time. Focusing on the role of symbolic communication in driving the development of more complex societies, he emphasizes that the emergence of human culture and language was not a linear process but one shaped by a complex interplay of biological, cultural, and environmental factors. See Deacon, *The Symbolic Species*. Cognitive psychologist and anthropologist Merlin Donald has also written extensively about the evolution of human

culture and brain cognition. He argues that human culture and cognition have evolved in three distinct stages—mimetic, mythic, and theoretic—and that this evolution was not linear but a co-evolutionary process, where the brain evolved to adapt to the demands of culture, which in turn drove the evolution of the brain. See Merlin Donald, *A Mind So Rare: The Evolution of Human Consciousness* (New York: W. W. Norton, 2001).

108. In the lecture series *Canticle to the Cosmos*, Brian Thomas Swimme discusses the profound archetypal relationships humans have inherited. One need only consider the fight-or-flight response or the mother-child bond to understand that relationships are not wholly created or maintained by individual humans. Instead, entering into a relationship awakens and invites us to participate in vast depths of what Swimme calls "transensual" energy. See Swimme's lecture "Episode 9: Fire in the Mind," Center for the Story of the Universe, https://storyoftheuniverse.org/videos/canticle-to-the-cosmos/.

109. Romanian historian of religion and philosopher Mircea Eliade uses the term "strong time before time" to describe an experience of time as "cyclical" or "eternal" rather than as linear and irreversible. See Mircea Eliade, *The Myth of the Eternal Return* (New York: Harper and Row, 1963). According to Eliade, traditional myths invoke a strong time to transcend the perishability and monotony of everyday life and reconnect us to the sacred depth of original creation. Leading theologian John F. Haught argues that the longing to return to origins continues to haunt both contemporary religions and contemporary science. He writes, "Like our mythmaking ancestors, [we] are secretly in search of the strong time of beginnings." He continues, "Since there is no possibility of our literally going back that far in time, we may presently connect with cosmic origins by breaking present organisms and other objects down into their most elemental parts. By way of this analytical reduction, we hope to approximate what the universe looked like in the beginning." See John F. Haught, *God after Einstein: What's Really Going On in the Universe?* (New Haven, CT: Yale University Press, 2022), 85.

110. The British philosopher, mathematician, and logician Alfred North Whitehead was perhaps the first to use the English word "creativity" to describe the universe. Whitehead argues that the universe is not a fixed and unchanging reality but an ever-changing process of becoming where creativity is the ultimate explanation for all of reality. Creativity, for Whitehead, is "another rendering of the Aristotelian 'matter,' and of the modern 'neutral stuff.' … It is that ultimate notion of the highest generality at the base of actuality." See Alfred North Whitehead, *Process and Reality: An Essay in Cosmology*, corrected ed., David Ray Griffin and Donald W. Sherburne, eds. (New York: The Free Press, 1978), 31.

111. According to Teilhard, the universe can no longer be thought of as a static order but rather as a universe in process; a continuing, upslope trajectory of evolution and embryogenesis is fundamental to the complexification process the universe undergoes at all levels. He writes, "To our clearer vision the universe is no longer a State but a Process. The cosmos has become a Cosmogenesis." Teilhard de Chardin, *The Future of Man*, 261. Central to his vision is the "realiz[ation] and accept[ance] once and for all that each new being has and must have a *cosmic embryogenesis.*" "Life does not work by following a single thread, nor yet by fits and starts. It pushes forward its whole network at one and the same time." "[Like an] embryo fashioned in the womb that bears it …, each stage or each state is represented by a *different being.*" See Teilhard de Chardin, *The Phenomenon of Man*, 78, 171.

112. Philosopher of science Timothy E. Eastman attributes ontologically real status to both actuality and potentiality. He writes, "The real is constituted by both the actual and the possible or, more fully expressed, potential relations (*potentiae*)." See Timothy E. Eastman, *Untying the Gordian Knot: Process, Reality, and Context* (Lanham, MD: Lexington Books, 2020), 23. Alfred North Whitehead's philosophy of organism also provides a special "category of existence" to what he calls *eternal objects* or *pure potentials for the specific determination of fact.* He writes, "In the becoming of an actual entity, the *potential* unity of many entities in disjunctive diversity—actual and non-actual—acquires the *real* unity of the one actual entity; so that the actual entity is the real concrescence of many potentials." See Whitehead, *Process and Reality*, 22. Whitehead and Eastman each offer an integrative framework in which potentiality and actuality are mutually implicative, and emergent temporality is the fundamental ordering relation.

113. The turn to the creative imagination is one of nine experiential turns elucidated by Wolfgang Leidhold wherein "the subtle realm of inspiration gained an unprecedented dignity." He describes the fleeting nature of inspirations that arise in the mind and the resultant need for readily accessible paper as a method of capturing and creating a record of creative visions. He writes, "The novel practice of keeping diaries and journals required an inexpensive supply of paper. In Europe, paper manufacturing had gradually emerged since the end of the thirteenth century, when water-powered paper mills had been introduced to make the production process more efficient. Thus, the practice of diary-writing took an unprecedented boom since the days of the Renaissance." See Leidhold, *The History of Experience*, 212–13. It is worth noting that while the Italians played a vital role in improving and refining paper-making techniques in Europe, making it more widely available during the Renaissance, a Chinese court official of the Han Dynasty named Cai Lun is credited with the invention of paper as we know it today in 105 CE. See Totally History, "The Invention of Paper," https://totallyhistory.com/the-invention-of-paper/.

114. Thomas Berry asserts, "Awareness that the universe is more Cosmogenesis than cosmos might be the greatest change in human consciousness that has taken place since the awakening of the human mind in the Paleolithic Period." See Thomas Berry, *The Great Work: Our Way into the Future* (New York: Bell Tower, 2000), 190.

115. For their discovery of the cosmic microwave background radiation, Arno Penzias and Robert Wilson were awarded the Nobel Prize in Physics in 1978, a prize they split with Pyotr Leonidovich Kapitsa "for his basic inventions and discoveries in the area of low-temperature physics." Penzias and Wilson's discovery was a major milestone in the study of cosmology and has led to a much deeper understanding of the origin and evolution of the universe. See "The Nobel Prize in Physics 1978," NobelPrize.org, Nobel Prize Outreach AB 2023, October 6, 2023, https://www.nobelprize.org/prizes/physics/1978/summary/.

116. Teilhard de Chardin borrows Sir Julian Huxley's "striking expression" to describe humankind as *"nothing else than evolution become conscious of itself."* Inextricably connected in a vast process of unfolding in which all elements emerge from previous elements, the human is distinguishable from its ancestors by its access to self-conscious reflection. Self-conscious reflection is, according to Teilhard, "the power acquired by a consciousness of turning in on

itself as an object endowed with its own particular consistency and value: no longer only to know something—but to know itself, no longer only to know, but to know that it knows." See Teilhard de Chardin, *The Phenomenon of Man*, 221, 165.

117. A collection of essays that trace the evolution of administrative structures, from their early rudimentary forms in city-states to more complex systems in larger empires, is found in "The Organization of Power: Aspects of Bureaucracy in the Ancient Near East," edited by McGuire Gibson and Robert D. Biggs, 2nd ed., *Studies in Ancient Oriental Civilization* 46 (Chicago: The Oriental Institute of the University of Chicago), 1991. The essays in this volume cover a vast area, from the early Mesopotamian states to the empires of Assyria and Persia, and provide a multidisciplinary perspective, combining archaeological, epigraphic, and anthropological data for a comprehensive understanding of ancient bureaucracy.

118. While sea jellies do not possess the centralized brain or bilateral symmetry of a vertebrate, they have a radial symmetry organized around a central axis and a decentralized nervous system called a "nerve net." A network of nerve cells called ganglia are distributed across their extended body, allowing the collective to respond to stimuli from any direction and coordinate more complex movements. The sea jelly moves and responds to its environment as a coordinated whole. Learn more about jellyfish at Jellipedia, https://www.jellipedia.com.au/. See also note 28 this volume.

119. The Classical Greek thinker Aristotle used the concept of *telos* to refer to an entity's inherent purpose or final cause. His *Nicomachean Ethics* argues that everything possesses a *telos*, and, for humans, the *telos* is the "good life" and human flourishing, called *Eudaimonia*. It is achievable through virtuous and reasoned living. In *Physics*, Aristotle elaborates his philosophy of nature, introducing four senses of the word "cause": material, formal, efficient, and final. *Telos* is aligned closely with Aristotle's concept of final cause as "the sense of end or 'that for which the sake of which' a thing is done" (*Physics* 194b33–34). According to Aristotle, the intrinsic *telos* of an acorn is becoming a full-grown oak tree, just as the full-grown oak is the final cause of the acorn. See Aristotle and Richard McKeon, *The Basic Works of Aristotle* (New York: Random House, 1941).

120. Cahokia was a Native American city in what is now the state of Illinois, just across the Mississippi River from present-day St. Louis, Missouri. At its peak in the thirteenth century, Cahokia was one of the largest and most complex cities in North America, with a population estimated by archaeologists to be as many as forty thousand people. This population was comparable to contemporary European cities such as London and far exceeded that of contemporary Paris. See Glenn Hodges, "America's Forgotten City," *National Geographic*, January 2011, https://www.nationalgeographic.com/magazine/article/americas-forgotten-city.

121. The Maya writing system—and Mesoamerican writing systems in general—is widely believed by scholars to have developed independently of writing systems in other parts of the world, such as those in Egypt, Mesopotamia, China, and the Indus Valley. While there were multiple writing systems in Mesoamerica (like the Zapotec and Epi-Olmec scripts), they share a common ancestry that evolved and was refined over centuries within

the context of Mesoamerican cultures and civilizations. Archaeologist Michael D. Coe of Yale University is a pioneering expert on the Olmec civilization and author of *Breaking the Mayan Code*. See Michael D. Coe, *Breaking the Maya Code* (New York: Thames and Hudson, 1992). Transcripts of filmed interviews with Coe regarding the origins of the Mayan writing systems, the nature of writing systems in general, and a wealth of other topics can be found at Night Fire Films, https://nightfirefilms.org/breaking-the-maya-code/interview-archives/.

122. James Gleick's seminal work, *Chaos: Making a New Science*, is an excellent general-audience resource for the concepts and histories of chaos theory, including "basins of attraction." In dynamical systems, a "basin of attraction" defines the set of starting conditions leading to a specific stable behavior or state called an "attractor." Attractors are end-states toward which a system evolves. If a system begins within a basin of attraction, it will eventually reach its associated attractor, regardless of minor disturbances. This concept is key in nonlinear dynamics and chaos theory, indicating how initial conditions influence long-term outcomes. See James Gleick, *Chaos: Making a New Science* (New York: Penguin Books, 1987).

123. The phase transition of crystallization is a common phenomenon in many areas of science and technology, including chemistry, materials science, and food science. James Gleick writes,

> Like so much of chaos itself, phase transitions involve a kind of macroscopic behavior that seems hard to predict by looking at the microscopic details. When a solid is heated, its molecules vibrate with added energy. They push outward against their bonds and force the substance to expand. The more heat, the more expansion. Yet, at a certain temperature and pressure, the change becomes sudden and discontinuous. A rope has been stretching; now it breaks.... The average atomic energy has barely changed, but the material—now a liquid, or a magnet, or a superconductor—has entered a new realm.

Gleick, *Chaos*, 127.

124. Jared Diamond has written an important book in the emerging field of collapseology that underscores the disaster of "overspending Earth's environmental capital." See Jared Diamond, *Collapse: How Societies Choose to Fail or Succeed* (New York: Penguin Books, 2011). Though cautiously optimistic, he fears our fate is determined by the dangerous overuse of limited fossil fuels, soils, and forest ecosystems, among other natural "resources." William Rees emphasizes that Diamond's book is "a necessary antidote" to the view that environmental problems are largely hoaxes and the human future secure. Rees writes,

> Human behavior towards the ecosphere has become dysfunctional and now arguably threatens our long-term security. The real problem is that the modern world remains in the sway of a dangerously illusory cultural myth.... Most governments and international agencies seem to believe that the human enterprise is somehow "decoupling" from the environment and thus poised for unlimited expansion. Jared Diamond's new book, *Collapse*, confronts this contradiction head-on.

See William Rees, "Contemplating the Abyss: The Role of Environmental Degradation in the Collapse of Human Societies," *Nature* 433, no. 7021 (2005): 15–16, https://www.nature.com/articles/433015a.

125. See Jutta Bolt and Jan Luiten van Zanden, "Maddison Style Estimates of the Evolution of the World Economy: A New 2020 Update," Maddison Project Database, version 2020, chrome-extension://efaidnbmnnnibpcajpcglclefindmkaj/https://www.rug.nl/ggdc/historicaldevelopment/maddison/publications/wp15.pdf.

126. Here, the writers use the word "learn" in much the same sense as Teilhard used the word "seeing" in the *Foreword* to his book *The Phenomenon of Man.* Teilhard writes,

> *Seeing.* We might say that the whole of life lies in that verb—if not ultimately, at least essentially. Fuller being is closer union.... But let us emphasize the point: union increases only through an increase in consciousness, that is to say in vision. And that, doubtless, is why the history of the living world can be summarized as the elaboration of ever more perfect eyes within a cosmos in which there is always something more to be seen.... To try to see more and better is not a matter of whim or curiosity or self-indulgence. *To see or to perish* is the very condition laid upon everything that makes up the universe, by reason of the mysterious gift of existence. And this, in superior measure, is man's condition.

See Teilhard de Chardin, *The Phenomenon of Man*, 31. The word "seeing," for Teilhard, also involves the advancing and expression of something hitherto concealed beyond physical determinisms. He writes, "Beings come together to prolong not themselves but what they have gained.... Love is an adventure and a conquest. It survives and develops, like the universe itself, only by perpetual discovery." See Teilhard de Chardin, *Human Energy*, 73–74.

127. The so-called three-body problem, discovered by the brilliant French mathematician, philosopher, and physicist Henri Poincaré in 1890, concerns the fundamental impossibility of predicting the motion of three or more objects mutually attracted by gravity. With just two celestial bodies interacting gravitationally, the exact future movement of both can be determined using Newton's mathematical equations. However, when a third body is added to the system, the motion resulting from their gravitational interaction cannot be worked out exactly; a series of approximations are required to "close in" on the mathematical solution. Henri Poincaré proved there is no general analytic solution to the three-body problem. Three-body and many-body systems, which characterize natural world systems, are chaotic and unpredictable in the long term, suggesting reductionism per se is an illusion. For an intriguing account of how the central configurations of shape spheres (corresponding to LaGrange points) in modern dynamical systems have led to exciting headway on the three-body problem, see Richard Montgomery, "The Three-Body Problem," *Scientific American* 321, no. 2 (August 2019): 66–73, https://www.scientificamerican.com/article/the-three-body-problem/.

128. In Whitehead's metaphysical framework, dispersal and contraction are fundamental, dynamic, and interdependent processes intrinsic to the ongoing creative evolution of reality. He introduces the notion of an "actual occasion" as the fundamental building block of reality, a "coming together" of dispersed elements to form a new whole.

Each actual occasion is characterized by its unique perspective, which Whitehead refers to as its "subjective form of prehension" and the "superject," which describes the objective aspect of an actual occasion. *Contraction* is the process through which the fragmented parts of reality are brought into relationships and organized into coherent structures. Whitehead, *Process and Reality*, 45.

129. We are not claiming that the James Webb Space Telescope has sentience, which is the ability to experience feelings and sensations. See "sentience," *Merriam-Webster Dictionary*, accessed March 18, 2024, https://www.merriam-webster.com/dictionary/sentience. However, the humans who developed the scope have sentience, and the Webb scope's revolutionary capabilities, especially pertaining to infrared observations, permit the observation of the earliest galaxies, something the Hubble scope could not do. For a comparison of the unique capacities of the James Webb Space Telescope to the capabilities of the Hubble Telescope and the Herschel Space Observatory, see James Webb Space Telescope, "Webb vs Hubble Telescope," https://webb.nasa.gov/content/about/comparisonWebbVsHubble.html.

130. Teilhard calls his philosophical orientation "hyperphysics" because it is beyond a material understanding of the universe; he chooses the word "hyperphysics" instead of "metaphysics" because the subject matter is not above or beyond being, but *more* being. Also, see note 75.

131. Teilhard de Chardin considers convergence to be a new law of nature that has come into being with the advent of reflective consciousness in humankind. See note 103.

132. For Pierre Teilhard de Chardin, convergence brings about centrated complexification whereby "individual elements must group and tighten not merely without becoming distorted in the process, but with an enhancement of their 'centric' qualities, i.e. their personality." Mutual internal affinity drives union and the novel emergence of ever more complex modes of being everywhere in the universe. Teilhard de Chardin specifically denounces any kind of top-down or totalitarian rule from above. It is only mutual internal affinity that "brings individuals together, not superficially and tangentially, but center to center." Only union through love "can physically possess the property of not merely differentiating but also personalizing the elements which comprise it." He writes, "Union differentiates, as I have said; the first result being that it endows a convergent Universe with the power to extend the individual fibers that compose it without their being lost in the whole." See Teilhard de Chardin, *The Future of Man*.

133. See Timothy E. Eastman, *Untying the Gordian Knot: Process, Reality, and Context* (Lanham, MD: Lexington Books, 2020).

134. In Whitehead's thought, two categories of existence "stand out with a certain extreme finality": actual entities and eternal objects, or pure potentials. See Whitehead, *Process and Reality*, 22.